THE JOURNEY OF A LIFETIME

A 90 day Devotion and Bible reading
plan that will change how you see
God, yourself, and the world.

Rev. Dr. Larry Oksten

This book is completed for two reasons. First, is for some reason God gave me the nudge to share these ideas. Second, Ginny you have pushed me and supported me over the years. A book was something we always talked aboiut and here it is. Thank you. I love you.

CONTENTS

INTRODUCTION

Introduction: Why are we here?

Why are we here? This book is my attempt to help folks take a 90-day journey through the Bible. So many people have read through the Bible in a year, and that can be challenging. In 90 days? Yes, difficult but so very rewarding as well. Each day will start with a reading, and then there is a devotion as well.

Read the devotion before or after you read the scripture for the day. The choice is yours. I write each one after the daily readings, but there are no rules here. As I am sitting here looking at my screen, there are two questions that keep rising up.

First, why does this need to be written?

Second, why are you the one that needs to write it?

For the longest time, I have waited to write this introduction. Everything else is basically written at this point. Yet, I waited until now to write this because I needed to be sure. I wanted to be sure that what I was doing made sense. I wanted to ensure that what I was doing mattered. This has probably been done by many other people over the years. It is not a unique endeavor, and I am sure it is not the best version of what has been done.

So why now and why me? I thought a lot about this, and I have figured out how to answer it. Years ago, I was a St. James High School student in Carney's Pt., New Jersey. One year, I took a journalism class with Mr. Fran Masciulli. I don't remember much about the course, but I remember one lesson. He told us that all articles that we wrote should answer six basic questions:

Who?

What?

Where?

When?

Why?

 How?

I think I am going to use his advice to help answer why we are both here. I am going to answer these questions to help you understand why I write.

Who?

 As you probably know from the front cover of the book, my name is Larry Oksten. I am an ordained pastor in the United Methodist Church and have been for about 20 years now. I grew up Roman Catholic. I went to Catholic School from grades one through my high school graduation. After high school, I didn't attend church for over ten years. My wife and I got married in the United Methodist Church because she grew up in that tradition. From there, it was a short little journey until I became a pastor. Not really, but that is for another book! So this is why I write.

What?

This question is a bit tricky. What am I trying to do with this book? As I stated, I know this isn't a unique book. There have been others, I am sure. Yet, I think what I bring is something different than other authors. I want to help you see the Bible like I see the Bible.

I believe that God has done everything possible to make these words come to life for us. Yet, we seem to make it difficult to understand or live out. My devotions accompanying each day's reading are my way to pick out something that will stick with you. They are simple stories or thoughts that will enable you to see the words come to life in new ways. So this is why I write.

Where?

Typically, this question is journalism's way to capture the location that the events happened. For me, it is a bit different. It is about where I am in my life. I am a pastor who has seen people struggle for almost 2 years from a global pandemic. We are not where we were pre-pandemic. There is a lack of trust that did not exist before. There is a level of fear, doubt, and anger that exists as well.

I am struck by the potential that the Bible has to bring calm and hope to a world that desperately needs it. So, where are we? Right where God is at work, and for me, that is an excellent place to be. So this is why I write.

When?

Time is the one thing that is the same for all of us. 24 hours is all we get each day. So what do we do with that time? For me, I realize that I have wasted a lot of hours in my life. There is so much that needs to be said and shared about the story of God. The time is now. So this is why I write.

Why?

I think this may be the most straightforward question. I write this because I believe the Bible is one way for us to know the mind and heart of God. There is not any "secret sauce" in there. Jesus says it best... "Love God...Love Others".

The Bible teaches us the extremes God will go to help us see how much we are loved. I want you to understand this in such a profound way you can't help but be changed by it. So this is why I write.

How?

This question is really about you. How do you approach this exercise? Because make no mistake, what you are about to undertake is not easy. Reading the Bible in 90 days may have been one of the most challenging projects I have ever undertaken. Yet, here is what I know, you can do it. I say that because I did it.

There are going to be challenges along the way. I want to give you advice that I hope you will take it to heart. Keep going. It is okay if you miss a day, don't let that stop you. If this 90-day journey becomes 100 days, that is okay. Keep going. Every day's reading is extensive, and that is okay. I have faith in you.

Have a plan and be faithful to it. Find a spot in your house where you can focus on the reading. After you are done with the reading, open up this book and read the devotion for the day. Some may help you clarify a point that you read. Some days you may disagree and think I am crazy. That is okay as well. Keep going. If you miss a day, start from where you left off the next day. I promise you that you can do this. If you need a pep talk as you go through it, please email me pastorbluejeans@me.com. I will answer you and can become your cheer

leader through this process. This 90 day (or however many days it takes you) will change you. I guarantee you.

DAY 1 – IT BEGINS

Today's Reading: Genesis 1: Genesis 16:6

"The Lord had said to Abram, "Go from your country, your people and your father's household to the land I will show you."
Genesis 12:1

Adam, Eve, Cain, Noah, Abram, Lot, and Sarai were journeyers. They left the land they knew and headed out to a different life. God's call on their life sent them out to the unknown. As I sit here today, I begin my own journey. It is also unknown. I know what I want to do; after all, I posted it on Facebook for all the world to see. The question for me becomes will I continue?

January 1st has become that date we have claimed in our culture as the day of new beginnings. Gyms will be packed, and healthy cooking shows will be watched. We all have good intentions, it seems. So how do you go from good intentions to good results? It is a question I ask myself often. I guess the first thing to understand is that January 1st, does not have to be the only day for new beginnings. It can be any day. It can be right now.

Perhaps the answer can be found by listening to the Winter Warlock. One foot, one chapter, one push-up, one vegetable, one piece of fruit after another. Adam and Eve did it even after losing a son. Cain did it despite killing his brother. Noah and his family took that step despite what I am sure was scorn and mocking from others. Abram and Sarai went as well. Each was seeking their own promised land.

So what will be my promised land this year? How about you? For me, I just want to be better. A better disciple, husband, father, friend, and oh yeah, a pastor. So today, my journey starts. Do you want to come along for the ride?

DAY 2 – THE JOURNEY CONTINUES

Today's Reading: Genesis 17:1 – Genesis 28:19

"Your descendants will be like the dust of the earth, and you will spread out to the west and to the east, to the north and to the south. All peoples on earth will be blessed through you and your offspring. I am with you and will watch over you wherever you go"
Genesis 28:14-15

God's plans. Just the phrase can be an intimidating or even stifling thing to think about. Does God have everything mapped out? Do I have a choice? Is there any room for my will or my desires? These are things, that if we are honest, we all must struggle with.

As I was reading through the scripture this morning, I began to see it in another way. God has a plan for us; it is the plan that was revealed to Abraham and restated through each patriarch we encounter, "Be a blessing" (give a lift). So if this is the plan God lays out for us, I believe we can see the room for our will and desire.

It starts with how we respond to God's plan. Will we strive to find ways to give a lift to the world, or will we simply focus on ourselves. The patriarchs and matriarchs were not merely men and women who boldly followed God; we see glimpses of selfishness, anger, and deception. They often times chose to not lift up but instead repress others.

Yet through it all, we see God remaining steadfast. God pushes and calls us to see the world how God sees it. Will we turn our eyes to the need or turn them away and instead focus on our own desires? As we continue this journey together, I take comfort in the stumbling I see from many in the book of Genesis.

See, I can relate. I don't have it all together. I know some look at me and see "PASTOR" and think that this means I have no struggles or pain. Perhaps some have decided to hold me to some higher standard. But, in the end, I am just a guy. A guy who has good intentions but often messes up. I need God's grace just like everyone else.

For me, this is not just the good news I find in the biblical story but the GOOD NEWS. The GOOD NEWS is that God knows me and all my faults and still loves me. God has that same great plan for you.

Ain't that some great, GOOD NEWS!

DAY 3 – USING GOD

Today's Reading: Genesis 28:20 – Genesis 40:11

"Jacob's sons replied deceitfully as they spoke to Shechem and his father Hamor."
Genesis 34:13

It's a funny thing watching people sometimes. We can justify almost anything, it seems. Suppose we want something badly enough or think we deserve something. In that case, we have no problem at all doing whatever is necessary to get it. So is it any wonder we often find ourselves in the messes we are in?

Jacob had a daughter named Dinah. Dinah's story is one of several in Genesis that shows up seemingly out of place and interrupts the narrative. However, these interruptions are often some of the most critical stories in Genesis. This one is no exception.

For those who have not done the reading yet today, I don't want to focus on what happened to poor Dinah. Instead, as I was reading this morning, I was struck by how her brothers responded.

As we continue reading Genesis this morning, we learn that they are scheming to begin with and somewhat impulsive. We see a glimpse of that here. We see also how they use God, or their faith, to cause and violence. Their actions are sudden and lethal.

Do you want to be one of the "GodUsers," or do you want to be used by God? It seems like a simple enough choice, but history suggests it isn't always that clear-cut. If we strive to be used by God instead of being a "GodUser," we need to make time for

God. We need to spend time in worship, prayer, fellowship, and mission.

I think in many ways, it simply breaks down to my trust level. Do I trust God to be God, or do I think God needs help doing the job? If I trust God to be God, it will then allow me to be me. The person created in the "imago Dei." I like the idea of me living out that image much better than trying to recreate that image.

Let's allow God to use us today!

DAY 4 – LOOK AROUND YOU

Today's Reading: Genesis 40:12 – Genesis 50:26

"Then Pharaoh said to Joseph, "I am Pharaoh, but without your word no one will lift hand or foot in all Egypt."Pharaoh gave Joseph the name Zaphenath-Paneah"

Genesis 41: 44-45

Watching a child experience something for the very first time is a fantastic thing. The wonder and excitement that they exhibit on their faces are astounding. They take it all in and just marvel at the newness of it all. So what do you think happens to us when we get older?
Somewhere along the way, we lose that ability. We call it maturing as we begin to look at the world in more discerning and discriminating ways. We create labels for things to determine what is "good" and what is "bad." Our time is often spent assigning items to certain boxes which have these labels on them. It is a way to make the world safer and easier to understand, I believe.

What if?

What if, instead of creating labels, we went back to how we used to be. Taking in all that we see and seeing it again as if it was the first time. Perhaps we have missed something. Maybe we can see things and experience things in a new way. But, would it be that difficult?

I ask this question because as I finished reading the book of

Genesis this morning, I couldn't help but marvel at Zaphenath-Paneah. Of course, he had to learn to look at things in a new way. He had to re-label stuff, perhaps. But, he was given the ability to do something and see things differently. Even starting with his name, after all, we know Zaphenath-Paneah as Joseph, son of Jacob.

Joseph was a Jewish boy who was forced to see things differently. Forced to see his captors and jailers and real people, not monsters. He was forced to see and understand new customs and cultures and adopt them somehow as his own. He was forced to see the brothers who betrayed him as brothers that he loved. Yet, in every situation, he thrived. It must have been difficult.

I think he was only able to do it because of his foundation in God. Looking around and seeing the world differently and not as we are "supposed" to often takes courage and faith. It is courage and faith-based on God. Joseph understood that his God was bigger than any label or in any way he had known. It gave him the freedom to look at the world in new ways.

So what labels or boxes is God challenging you to look at differently? Is your God big enough to handle that? Mine is!

DAY 5 – POWER UP

Today's Reading: Exodus 1:1 – Exodus 15:19

"What about your brother, Aaron the Levite? I know he can speak well. He is already on his way to meet you, and he will be glad to see you."
Exodus 4:14

I have been watching my youngest son play a lot of Super Mario recently. As I was reading through the first 15 chapters of Exodus this morning, I could not help but think a lot about Mario and his brother Luigi. There are a lot of life lessons to be learned from those two.

Mario and Luigi find themselves in many crazy situations. They explore different worlds and encounter trouble. The brothers work together to accomplish goals and to move on to the next level. However, reality sets in for them both, and after a series of mishaps, Luigi and/or Mario die. Yet, something magical happens in the game. If you are playing the correct version of the game, Luigi and Mario have unlimited power-ups. In other words, the brothers are unstoppable together!

I thought a lot about Mario and Luigi as I read this morning because of the brothers. Aaron and Moses were the ancient precursors for Mario and Luigi. They worked together like a fine-tuned machine. Moses did not believe he could do what God was calling him to do, so God told him to rely on Aaron. Together, with the power of God, they went face to face with Pharaoh and won.

We all need a Luigi or Aaron in our lives. Someone who can help us wrestle with what God is calling us to do. Someone who is there to face off against whatever giants may come. A person to walk with us through the ups and downs.

Our Luigi will be a person who brings power to us when we are beaten down. It will be a person who will not let us wallow in the murk and mire alone. The great news is we get to play the role of Luigi for that person as well. This relationship is mutually beneficial.

God has something he is trying to help us see. Perhaps it is some journey we need to go on. Maybe it is something we need to stand up to or someone we need to stand up for. Whatever it is, God is also going to provide our own Aaron or Luigi for the trip. So keep moving and keep your eyes open; your power-up is coming.

DAY 6 – SOME SERIOUS CLOWNING AROUND

Today's Reading: Exodus 15:19 – Exodus 28:43

"Do not oppress a foreigner; you yourselves know how it feels to be foreigners, because you were foreigners in Egypt."
Genesis 23:9

As I read through the chapters in Exodus this morning, I couldn't help but think about clowns. For about two years, we were enmeshed in a process at the church I was serving. This process was something we came to know as the C.L.O.W.N. Squad. C.L.O.W.N. is an acronym that stands for Creatively Loving Our Wonderful Neighbors. The main thrust of this was the idea of community. We all want it, and we all need it.

Community and relationships are something that we all seek. The only question is, what type of community and relationship are we going to pursue? At the heart of our conversation, we focused on the fact that everybody matters and everybody is worthy because we are ALL children of God. Having the identity of a child of God is something that changes everything or at least should.

In Exodus this morning, we read about laws, commands, and plans. We know some of these laws as the 10 Commandments. Others of them might not have been as familiar. However, as I read, I couldn't help but think of the world today. We are in such disarray. We have demonstrations, violence, civil unrest, and anger pervasive, it seems.

These chapters in Exodus are God's plan to help elevate us. Through Moses, it is God's way to once again remind us that we matter...we ALL matter. My eye is as valuable as yours. Your oxen are as valuable as mine. Take care of your parents and value the stranger. These seem to be basic things and perhaps not worth mentioning at first glance.

Instead, this is the exact thing the Israelites needed to hear. God was sharing his vision with them. They were in the midst of a journey of epic proportions. Their life would be different, but they were unsure what it would and should look like. God was laying down the foundation.

As we look at our world, we, too, are on an epic journey. We are moving forward together, and the question becomes where we are headed and what we will look like when we get there. Let's go back to the basics and remember how valued we are in God's eyes. Then, we can begin to recapture that idea of authentic community and relationship.

So let's start clowning around...together!

DAY 7 – TEMPORARY DIGS...OR NOT

Today's Reading: Exodus 29:1 – Exodus 40:38

"In all the travels of the Israelites, whenever the cloud lifted from above the tabernacle, they would set out; but if the cloud did not lift, they did not set out—until the day it lifted"

When I was in the army, we did a lot of training. Much of the activity consisted of us with rucksacks on our backs. On or attached to the rucksacks, we always would have a bedroll and an e-tool. The e-tool, an entrenching tool, was a collapsible shovel. We used it to dig trenches around our tents. We also used it to help and/or create various things we would need in our time in the field.

These were just temporary structures, holes, and trenches. We needed them while we were settled down for a while but not once we left. We moved on the next day and then started the digging again once we settled in again. We learned to move quickly and efficiently. We knew that we would have the tools, talent, and time to have what we needed each day when we arrived at our destination. This gave us peace of mind.

The Israelites might not have been in the army, but they were doing their own fair share of setting up, breaking down and traveling. We are unsure if the Israelites had their own e-tool, but we know they had something even more critical. They were traveling with God. So, God had Moses create a "temporary dwelling" that would be set up and taken down as the Israelites set up or broke down camp.

This was the place where the presence of God would be apparent to the people. This was the beginning, in many ways, with our attempt to box up God, I believe. The thinking can be that if we know where God is and can be assured of his presence there, perhaps we are "off the hook" in other places. In my mind, this was always the beginning of the secular vs. holy argument.

I have always struggled with this. I believe Paul makes it quite clear in his writing that within US resides the resting place of God. If this is the case, then we are never in a secular place; we are always in a holy place as it all belongs to God. There is nothing temporary about the Spirit of God for God's people.

Look around today, in the midst of all you see, God is there. In the midst of the pain and suffering, God is there. In joy and happiness, God is there.
God is there. Isn't that a great thing!

\

DAY 8 – IT'S MESSY BUSINESS

Today's Reading: Leviticus 1:1 – Leviticus 14:32

"Then Moses said, 'This is what the Lord has commanded you to do, so that the glory of the Lord may appear to you.' "
Leviticus 9:6

If I have learned anything in my 48 plus years in life, it is that community is messy. When you get a couple of people together trying to accomplish anything, the one thing you can be sure of is that it is not going to be simple. Two people often mean at least two different ideas or sets of priorities. As you continue to add people to the mess that happens due to the mix, the number of views and priorities increases exponentially.

Moses and Aaron, and God are dealing with just that fact as we move on into the book of Leviticus. The Israelites have moved on to a new place in their journey from captivity to freedom in God. As they continue, God is establishing the expectations of the new community. There will be problems, and there will be in, and God is acknowledging that fact.

For some people, establishing rules and standards are walls that inhibit people and make life oppressive. I was reading "Orthodoxy" by G.K. Chesterton today, and he spoke about this idea. He was talking about Christian doctrine, which can be defined as rules and standards. He said, "Doctrine may be walls, but it is the walls of a playground." I love this!

The Israelites needed the walls set up, but they were allowed to play and enjoy life within the protection of the borders. It is the same with us. We have standards and rules and laws that we are called to live by. These laws are established by the government, church, family, business. However, these standards help us to create community. Yet, within those standards and rules, there is still lots of time to play and enjoy.

So enjoy the mess as you strive towards community. Live a life of freedom that comes from knowing that release comes from knowing and walking with God.

DAY 9 – DANGER!

Today's Reading: Leviticus 14:33 – Leviticus 26:26

"Keep all my decrees and all my laws and follow them. I am the Lord."
Leviticus 19:37

I remember the moment that my life was no longer going to be the same. It was about 3 a.m. I was in some unknown, to me, part of Oklahoma. I was awakened by yelling and doors slamming. I was lying down on a top bunk, and the next thing I knew, I was standing at attention as several men were screaming in my face. Army basic training had started.

There are several rules for basic training, but I think that the one that resonates with me as I read the chapters in Leviticus this morning was separation. Part of the design in basic training is to isolate you from everything you know and retrain you. The army then tries to impart the values and skillset that you will need to be the person they need you to be.

As Moses was continuing to lead his people, God was giving them a window. It was a window that allowed them to see how those outside the community lived. This behavior was what God was deemed dangerous and unhealthy for the survival of the Israelite community. God was helping them create the skill set they needed to be vital in their new environment.

We need to see the world as it is, both good and bad. In the seeing of the world, we can find ways to engage in the world and live in the world as God has called us to live. God's world is beautiful and made to enjoy but can also be dangerous if we are not aware. So we find ourselves in this delicate place where we need to understand and live in but not be totally transformed from the world. Yet, we also need to ensure that we do not isolate ourselves from the world either.

So, open your eyes and your ears. See and listen to what the world is doing and saying. At the same time, look and listen to what God is doing and saying. God desires the best for us and has given us the best. The question is simply what will you give to God.

DAY 10 – IT'S ALL IN THE DETAILS

Today's Reading: Leviticus 26:27 – Numbers 8:4

"The Lord said to Moses and Aaron: 'The Israelites are to camp around the tent of meeting some distance from it, each of them under their standard and holding the banners of their family. ' "
Numbers 2: 1-2

We had just finished a Little League All-Star Game, and we were celebrating at Don and Bert's Custard Stand in Paulsboro. I thought Don and Bert's had the best cheeseburgers and fries, and I couldn't wait to order mine. I got my order, and before anyone could "steal" my food, I ran off to the car. I climbed into the station wagon and started chowing down.

Soon, I began to hear laughs from outside the car. I didn't stop to see what was so funny because my burger was so good. Eventually, I couldn't help but notice almost every teammate was surrounding the car I was in and laughing. Finally, I stopped eating long enough to roll down the window and see what was so funny. It was hard to discern through the laughing, but it seemed as if I was not in the coach's car. In fact, I was not in any car that was from the team. I was chowing down in a total stranger's car.

I intended to get to my meal, that I missed the vital detail of whose car I was getting into. I became so focused on what I thought the end result should be that I lost track of my journey. It seemed as if my planning stopped as soon as I could smell the burger and fries in the bag I was holding. I had lost perspective.

The Israelites were headed to the promised land, but they needed a plan. Many people needed to have some organization and some idea of what the expectations would be for them. In the first chapters of the book of Numbers, we begin to see those details develop. We see where they will stay and what some responsibilities will be for them.

As we read through these chapters, it is easy to miss the importance and plow right through them. Yet, in the details that are being laid out, we see the community starting to get some real foundation. We know how the plans made in the present can lead to a successful future.

It is those details and that planning that can ensure that the car you are in as you are eating your long-awaited burger is, in fact, the car you are supposed to be in.

It's all in the Details!

DAY 11 – GETTING FRUSTRATED

Today's Reading: Numbers 8:5 – Numbers 21:7

"Why did you bring us up out of Egypt to this terrible place? It has no grain or figs, grapevines or pomegranates. And there is no water to drink!'
Numbers 20:5

Haven't we all been there? Tired? Spent? Frustrated? Even a little angry? Wondering to ourselves whether any of it was worth it? I think, at one point or another, most of us have been there. Struggling to figure out whether anyone has been paying even a little bit of attention.

Moses was there. "We are hungry." "We are thirsty." "Why did you bring us here just to die in the desert"? He had heard it all before, and he had reached his breaking point. He was tired of being a scapegoat. He was tired of being challenged. Perhaps, he was even tired of God not acting as quickly as Moses wanted him to work. He had had enough,

So can we really blame him? Here he was again…standing before the rock. God's commands were pretty clear…" speak to the rock, and it will produce water." As the scene is presented, we can feel the frustration grow. Moses wants to put a slight emphasis on this. He wants the Israelites to know and God to know; this is getting old. So Moses strikes the rock twice, and to paraphrase that great sitcom, Seinfeld… "No Promised land for you!".

What rock is standing between you and God's promises today?

Are you struggling to see God's blessings because you can't see past the obstacles (rock) in your own life? Take some time today and do what Moses perhaps should have done. Take a deep breath. Say a prayer. Ask God for strength and move forward in trust.

Maybe it really can be that easy. Are you ready to try?

DAY 12 - LOST IN THE FOG

Today's Reading: Numbers 21:8 – Numbers 32:19

"Moses and Eleazar the priest accepted from them the gold—all the crafted articles."
Numbers 31:51

We have all had the experience of traveling in a fog. It can be very disorientating. What do we see, and what don't we see? Hearing sounds in the fog can be a little problematic as well. Some sounds are amplified, and others are silenced. For many, fog is simply not fun.

As I read these passages in the Old Testament, I must admit that I often feel like I am foggy. These passages are not clear to me in the fog created through context, time, and culture. I struggle to see the shape of God and hear the voice of God while I read these chapters.
So sitting in the fog, I have decisions to make. I choose God. I prefer that no matter what I see and what I read, God is alive and is not leaving me to my own devices in the fog. For that, I am eternally grateful. So, together with God, I seek direction.

Today there is no deep insight or witty stories to make a point. Today there is simply trust. I trust God. I do not always trust storytellers. I trust God more than I will trust people's motives and justifications.

I have nothing more this morning to say….I think I am going to go pray.

DAY 13 – WE TEACH THEM UP

Today's Reading: Numbers 32:20 – Deuteronomy 7:26

"These are the words Moses spoke to all Israel"
Deuteronomy 1:1

I come from a family that seemingly has teaching in its blood. Teachers and nurses, and others who have spent much of their adult life instructing others in many different ways. In many ways, this has shaped my views on the world. It has also helped me learn to see the importance of telling stories.

One way to teach and lead people is to help them learn the story they share and to help them learn to tell it. Unfortunately, an area in which we often fail the younger generation is by letting others help mold and form their story. We then end up not being part of that fundamental process. Yet, storytelling is a vital part of who we are. We all have a story to tell, and we all need others to help us shape that story.

Moses stood before the people of Israel and once again reminded them of their journey together. They stood at the precipice of the promised land, and now they needed one final storytelling lesson. Moses reminded them of where they had been and where they were now. He offered them one last story.

Are we taking the time to tell our story to others? Do we take the time to help others in their own storytelling? The answers to these questions become the key to whether we will have success as a family, community, and church. When we learn to tell the story, we can start to live out that story more and more each day.

Moses wasn't going to complete the trip into the promised land; his part was winding up. So he powerfully reminded the Israelites of the crucial moments, both good and bad, they shared. These stories would resonate in their hearts and minds, and they would be able to share them with future generations. In the retelling, the journey they shared remained alive.

As we continue reading the bible in #90days, let's once again relive this story together.

DAY 14 - THESE DAYS HAVE TAUGHT US ONE THING

Today's Reading Deuteronomy 8:1 – Deuteronomy 23:11

"Love the Lord your God and keep his requirements, his decrees, his laws and his commands always."
Deuteronomy 11:1

I am not very strong, but even I can tear a piece of paper. Yet, something happens as more and more paper is added to the pile. Eventually, it becomes too much for me to tear. This is the reality for every one of us. The number of pieces of paper needed will be different, but we all hit the limit at some point. It becomes too big a task to handle on our own.

The good news for us is that even when we have reached the limit, proverbially or literally, we are not alone. Moses 'speech to the Israelites, as they stood at the precipice of the promised land, could just as easily be directed towards us. Moses reminded the people, no matter where they went or where they might find themselves, that God was with them.

However, for that not to be just another cliché, we must really understand what that may mean for us. What does "God is with me" look like? Does it really make any difference? Is there any benefit for me? These are questions that we should look at closely.

"God is with me."

I need to open my eyes and look beyond, around, and often through whatever I am dealing with. When I can do that, I will find the strength, comfort, and peace that comes from God. My mind and spirit will be refreshed, and I will have the power to continue.

Does it really make any difference?

I think the biblical story is filled with the answer to that question. Abraham, Moses, Isaac, Jacob, Ruth, and David are just a few examples of people for who God's presence made a real difference. If we are truthful, we can all pinpoint times in our own lives where that has been the case.

Is there any benefit for me?

Yes, there is a benefit, but at times, it may not be clearly evident. However, as I read the chapters of Deuteronomy this morning, I once again was reminded of the benefit. God provides; comfort, resources, people, and hope. The advantage is that in whatever circumstance God has brought us to or we find ourselves in, we will discover what God has provided for us for that moment.
We are not alone; God is with us, and that is a great thing.

DAY 15 – AND TODAY, THEY HAD A HISTORY TEST

Today's Reading Deuteronomy 23:13 – Deuteronomy 32:14

"If you fully obey the Lord your God and carefully follow all his commands I give you today, the Lord your God will set you high above all the nations on earth. All these blessings will come on you and accompany you if you obey the Lord your God"
Deuteronomy 28: 1-2

As I write this, college is about to start back up for the semester. Throughout the town, the young people are coming back to campus. They are settling into dorms and preparing themselves for what is about to happen this semester. A last trip to the supermarket and perhaps the bookstore, and they will be ready to go.

But are they really ready? Have they gotten everything that they need, and are they prepared for the classes, professors, and assignments ahead? There is really one way to know that, and that is to go experience it. Preparation is essential and often times vital to our success. However, it is in the actual doing that we see how that preparation has paid off.

One final thing we can do to understand if we are prepared is to look back at history. How have we performed in the past? What have we done that has brought us success or failure in the past? What have we seen others do that have brought them success?

So again, we can look at many questions and try to help us prepare for what lies before us.

Looking back at how they got to where they are is where Moses finds himself in the final chapters of Deuteronomy. Moses and the Israelites had been on a long journey. They had seen the highs and the lows. Together they had been witnesses to the power of God. Now was time for the next step, the journey forward.

Moses is honoring the past and using it to prepare the people as they go into the unknown. The testing isn't over, and the lessons will continue. They will bring the lessons with them into the promised land and allow those lessons to assist them.
Prepare yourself...a test is coming...are you ready?

DAY 16 – LET'S TALK ABOUT SECRETS

Today's Reading Joshua 1:1 – Joshua 14:15

"Joshua tore his clothes and fell facedown to the ground before the ark of the Lord, remaining there till evening. The elders of Israel did the same, and sprinkled dust on their heads."
Joshua 7:6

Psst, I want to tell you a secret…

Secrets can kill ya. Now don't get me wrong, being able to trust people with a secret can be affirming. Knowing there is someone you can trust with something that can be harmful or embarrassing to you is a great feeling. Everyone should have people in their lives like that.
However, there are some secrets that we won't share or feel we can't share. So we hold on to them and try to carry the burden alone. The weight of the secret can become unbearable. Keeping the secret can become a full-time job. It can dominate our time and energy.

Achan had such a secret. He disobeyed God. He hid what he did from everyone, but God knew. Achan's secret destroyed his whole family once it came out. The thing about secrets is that carrying them has a price. So the question becomes, are we willing to pay it?
So if everyone has secrets and we realize they can be dangerous, what do we do?

1st: Trust God

God can handle it. Whatever it is. Share your burden and lighten your load.

2nd: Be honest with yourself
You can't fool yourself, nor can you fool God. So start with that, and it will make everything easier.

3rd: Learn who to count on
Everyone needs people that they can share their ups and downs AND secrets. Find people like that.

3 Simple things. None of them earth-shattering. However, they can help you avoid Achan's sin.

DAY 17 - WHY?
HERE IS A COUPLE
REASONS

Today's Reading Joshua 15:1 – Judges 3:27

"Again the Israelites did evil in the eyes of the Lord"
Judges 3:12

We have all seen them or perhaps even participated in them. The selfie phenomenon continues to grow; what started out as a teenage activity has spread through the world like wildfire. Men and women of all ages now find themselves getting into the selfie craze. It has gotten so pervasive that there are now products being created to help people take selfies:

What is the obsession?
What is the point?
What are we really saying about ourselves?

I think what we are seeing here is similar to what the people of Israel were dealing with as we read the book of Judges. The Israelites were focused on themselves. They wanted to be happy and content. So they were doing everything they could to ensure that happiness.

However, they neglected to care how their happiness was impacting others. They also were seemingly not concerned whether their actions were pleasing to God. God's reaction to the Israelite "selfie" craze was to put powerful kings in their way as opposition. God continued to try to get the Israelites attention.

So perhaps it is time to put down the "selfie stick" and look around. Who are you trying to please? Is it you? Are your actions and attitudes directed towards bringing you and you alone pleasure? I think it is time for a change.
Here are a few ways to bring the focus away from your "selfie" and back towards pleasing God today.

1. Put the phone down and pick up a bible.
2. Drop the phone from your hands and fold them together and pray.
3. Put the phone down and go help someone.
4. Turn the phone app off and call someone you haven't seen in a while and tell them you are praying for them
5. Put the phone down and spend time with your family and friends.
6. Put the phone away and spend time enjoying the beautiful creation God has provided.
7. Put the phone down and go read a classic book

Just a few ideas. There are so many others. But whatever you do, find ways to please God.

DAY 18 - THE WEAK AND THE STRONG

Today's Reading Judges 3:27 – Judges 15:12

" 'Watch me, follow my lead. When I get to the edge of the camp, do exactly as I do. When I and all who are with me blow our trumpets, then from all around the camp blow yours and shout, For the Lord and for Gideon.' "
Judges 7:17-18

Not much to say today, just a simple thought. Today's reading included the story of Gideon and part of the story of Samson. Two more different "heroes" we shall never meet. Gideon, when we meet him, is a little whiny and perhaps even manipulative. Samson is brash and arrogant with no concern for human life.

Yet, God used them both in mighty ways. I assume you are like me and have struggled with issues of self-doubt on occasion. Perhaps you feel as if you do not measure up to those around you. Maybe you think you are part of the "terrible Toos":
Too old
Too young
Too rich
Too poor
Too white
Too black
Too gay
Too straight
Too Methodist
Too Catholic

Too Agnostic
you get the point.

Gideon's story should be a trumpet call (see what I did there) to you. God knows you and still has an excellent plan for you. But don't get feeling so good about yourself that you catch the other part of the "Terrible Toos":
Too arrogant
Too prideful
Too boastful
Too angry
Too resentful

Again, you get the picture.
Go can use you too. However, God also will work to show you some humility and compassion. We are all valuable and worthy in the eyes of God.

DAY 19 – CHARACTER MATTERS

Today's Reading Judges 15:13 – 1 Samuel 2:29

"But Ruth replied, 'Don't urge me to leave you or to turn back from you. Where you go I will go, and where you stay I will stay. Your people will be my people and your God my God. Where you die I will die, and there I will be buried. May the Lord deal with me, be it ever so severely, if even death separates you and me.' When Naomi realized that Ruth was determined to go with her, she stopped urging her."

Ruth 1: 16-18

Character development, character programs, and character training are things that are widespread throughout our culture. Our schools invest much time and energy into the importance of developing good character in their students. We invest a lot of time and energy in promoting the importance of character.

Martin Luther King, Jr., was a man who exhibited character and lifted up a country. He was a man who helped people see that everyone matters and that color of the skin is not what counts. It is our hearts. It is the decisions we make when no one else is looking. This is where character is developed.

I thought a lot about character this morning as I read the scripture. We have so many examples of good and bad character present. We have Delilah, the people of Gibeah, and Peninnah as examples of people showing a lack of character. We then see Ruth, Hannah. and Boaz as people who show us great examples of character.

Character counts.

So what are you doing when no one is watching? What decisions are you making? These are the things that define you. Those are the moments that will impact you and your community for years to come. Martin Luther King Jr. knew that basic fact. So, have other people throughout history like Mahatma Gandhi, Clara Burton, and Nelson Mandela.

Take time today and give thanks to those men and women who have been a guiding influence in your life. Remember the life of MLK, Jr. Think back to decisions you have made in the last day, weeks, and month. Are there some you would do differently? What can you do to make sure that you do make better choices?

Finally, make today more than just another day. Find something you can do or say that can make a positive contribution.

DAY 20 - READING LEADS TO RISKY BEHAVIOR.

Today's Reading1 Samuel 2:30 – 1 Samuel 15:35

"But the people refused to listen to Samuel. 'No!' they said. 'We want a king over us. Then we will be like all the other nations, with a king to lead us and to go out before us and fight our battles.'"
1 Samuel 8: 19-20

Every day we begin with a series of choices starting at us about the day ahead. Those choices we make all have consequences attached to them. These consequences could be negative or positive or perhaps even neutral. So we wake up each day with risks ahead.

Learning how to mitigate those risks becomes very important. For Christians, what we learn when we read these stories in the bible is how vital obedience is. We see examples in 1 Samuel of what happens when people are not obedient and faithful to God. When choices that are made are counter to what God wants and desires for us.

Being obedient to God is something that must be chosen and lived out each and every day. Over time with prayer and practice, it can become a habit. The question becomes, are we willing to do the work necessary for it to become a habit? Are we ready to make choices, not for immediate gratification but instead to be faithful and pleasing to God?

Living is risky enough...let's lessen the risk. Let's follow God.

DAY 21 - FEAR
STILL EXISTS

Today's Reading1 Samuel 16:1 – 1 Samuel 28:19

"Saul was afraid of David, because the Lord was with David but had departed from Saul."
1 Samuel 18:12

"The enemy is fear. We think it is hate; but it is really fear." - Gandhi.

I absolutely love this quote from Gandhi. I find myself thinking a lot about it in the world we live in. We see so much hate, it seems. Over the years we have seen the atrocities committed in the world by groups like ISIS. We know the terror caused by the events in Afghanistan, while the events in Ferguson and New York and in other places in our country are not quite in our rear-view mirrors.

We quickly use the term hate to describe many of these and other events, but I think Gandhi has something here. First, I think the word fear is perfect. Fear is defined by dictionary.com as "a distressing emotion aroused by impending danger, evil, pain, etc., whether the threat is real or imagined; the feeling or condition of being afraid."

I focus on the "real or imagined" part of the definition. How much of the fear we feel is self-induced? We can fear people because of skin color, ethnicity, or religion. We also may be afraid of people because of our own insecurity; there are so many reasons we can fear people. We have to take the time to ensure we don't allow fear to take over our lives.

Saul was afraid of David, and David was afraid of Saul. Saul allowed his fear to turn into hate. David did not let that happen to him. He continued to trust God. David knew Saul was out to kill him and made plans based on that. However, David continued to follow God's direction. He continued to do what he was led to by God.

So how do we take David's lessons to heart?

What can we do with the fear that pops up in our own lives?

To quote the great Thinker and NFL Quarterback Aaron Rogers: R-E-L-A-X.

R – Realize God is in charge

E – Expect God's presence… God will never leave you

L – Let go of doubt and fear..grab on to faith and trust

A – Anticipate God's grace…

X – Xenos…which is a Greek word for the stranger or the guest. It is what God reminds us that we all once were. So care for the Xenos; don't fear them.

Take a deep breath and relax. It is going to be ok.

DAY 22 – WHO IS YOUR NATHAN?

Today's Reading 1 Samuel 28:20 – 2 Samuel 12:10

"Then Nathan said to David, "You are the man! This is what the Lord, the God of Israel, says"
2 Samuel 12:7

I remember one day sitting in Starbucks and getting ready to go to class. I was preparing to sit with my cohort. We would question each other and challenge each other. We would share our journey and the progress of our project. When we were done, we would then accept the critique of others.

Would it be easy? Of course not, but it would be necessary. We had traveled with these people for almost three years. We had shared together and struggled together, and we trusted each other.

We all need people in our lives who will hold us accountable when we are straying off course. We need people who we trust to instruct and correct us when needed. Those people are vital in our lives. But, when the correction happens, we also need to humbly listen and accept what is being said.

David needed Nathan. I needed my cohort. I need my wife. I need friends who can do that.

Who is your Nathan?

DAY 23 – SAVE ME FROM ME

Today's Reading 2 Samuel 12:11 – 2 Samuel 22:18

"The king was shaken. He went up to the room over the gateway and wept. As he went, he said: 'O my son Absalom! My son, my son Absalom! If only I had died instead of you—O Absalom, my son, my son'"
2 Samuel 18:33

Nathan's words to David that we talked about yesterday changed David's outlook and behavior. However, there were still lots of consequences for David's actions. David's family was going to implode. There were going to be widening cracks to appear in the people of Israel as well. We see all this playing out in the chapters from today.

God forgives of that, there is no doubt. However, we need to understand that often our behavior carries consequences that we might not really want to deal with. So what do we do? How do we stop bad things from happening? How do we respond when faced with dire circumstances of our own doing?

Give Thanks: God is with us and will not leave us.
No matter what we are going through, God will be with us. This brings assurance and peace.

Evaluate: What decision or actions of ours have led to this circumstance
Understanding what brought us to this place can help us avoid certain decisions or actions in the future.

Respond: Respond – Pray and Act.

We need to bathe everything in prayer and seek guidance from God. Then, follow that up with action and do something. It does not have to be something to "fix" or "correct" anything. Just focus on making some change.

We all make mistakes. We all do dumb things. The reality is we all need God to save us and often keep saving us from ourselves. Accepting that we are not perfect and realizing that we are not superheroes is an important step. Humbling ourselves before God and seeking guidance is an even better one.

Dear God...save me from me. Amen.

DAY 24 – ON THIS EPISODE OF ALL MY CHILDREN

Today's Reading 2 Samuel 22:19 – 1 Kings 7:37

"So give your servant a discerning heart to govern your people and to distinguish between right and wrong. For who is able to govern this great people of yours?"
1 Kings 3:9

You remember her, don't you? For decades she ran amok all throughout Pine Valley. It did not matter whether you were her friend or self-pronounced foe. What Erica Kane wanted, it seemed Erica Kane would get. She loved hard and hated harder. She tried to bring a little glamour to family dysfunction.

Make no mistake, there was a lot of dysfunction. But, perhaps that was part of the appeal of shows like All My Children, One Life to Live, and General Hospital (can you tell I was an ABC Soap guy). These shows brought some excitement and intrigue to what we all know is petty strife and family discord. Finally, we could see ourselves in the struggle. We root for people like Erica Kane, Adam Chandler, or Monica Quartermaine to dispense needed justice.

We eventually all learn that life is not Soap Opera, or is it? Reading these chapters in the Bible this morning, I was reminded of Pine Valley, Llanview, and Port Charles and those families' problems. The chapters this morning were about power, pride, and money. They spoke to the lengths people would go to to get what they wanted.

Whether reading the Bible or watching soap operas, I think we need to remember a few things. The first, that no matter what, people matter more than stuff. It seems as if we get caught up too quickly in a generation-long exercise in "money rules." The second, that people always matter more than things. We were created to be in relationship with each other, not to gather items.

As I read those chapters, I was encouraged by God's faithfulness. I was struck by Solomon's desire for wisdom. But, I was also reminded that even faithful people like Solomon do dumb things. So my goal today, don't do too many dumb things.

Not Erica Kane worthy... but I will take it!

DAY 25 – THE OCEAN WAS ANGRY, MY FRIENDS

Today's Reading 1 Kings 7:38 – 1 Kings 16:20

"Even after this, Jeroboam did not change his evil ways, but once more appointed priests for the high places from all sorts of people. Anyone who wanted to become a priest he consecrated for the high places."
1 Kings 13:33

We don't always get it right. We try...we really, really do. Yet, time and time again, we find ourselves falling short. Intentions are one thing, but actions are what we often use to judge others and ourselves. Take, for instance, the weather forecasters.

All throughout the Northeast, we were told to prepare for a Winter Storm that would be devastating. Throughout Philadelphia and New Jersey, travel bans were enacted, schools were closed, and businesses were shut down as people prepared to fight off the blizzard. Yet, I woke up and saw nothing as I expected.

The roads were pretty clear. The travel bans were being lifted, and soon life goes back to normal. They tried; they really, really did. But they just missed this forecast. Now I know there are parts of New England that had been blasted snow-wise. Yet, we escaped the storm.

Some of the Israelite kings tried as well. We read today of a few that really did try to follow the laws of God. Yet we are reminded that they ignored some areas, often the altars in the high places used to sacrifice to other gods. Those places were often still in use, and while the kings didn't notice them, God did. They perhaps were trying to be men of integrity but were falling short.

What places in our lives are we missing? Are there areas in our life that we are ignoring while we focus on other things? What can we do about that? Is there trouble looming for us in the high places of our lives?

Take some time today while you are snowed in if you are, and do some self-evaluation. Try and identify that area in your life that you may be lying to yourself about. For Seinfeld fans, we may remember the many exploits of George Costanza. But, unfortunately, his failure to really see himself and not be a man of integrity often put him in bad spots.

Don't let the angry oceans swirl in your life. Don't let the high areas go unattended.

DAY 26 - AND THEN THERE WAS SNOW!

Today's Reading 1 Kings 16:21 – 2 Kings 4:37

"When they had crossed, Elijah said to Elisha, 'Tell me, what can I do for you before I am taken from you?' 'Let me inherit a double portion of your spirit,' Elisha replied. "
2 Kings 2:9

When I wrote this my view was from the balcony of my room in Long Branch I was gathered with many colleagues for the Bishop's convocation for the Greater New Jersey Annual Conference. This would be a time of learning and fellowship for us over a couple of days.

According to the weather forecasts, we gathered together as the world around us prepared for a another storm of epic proportions. We talked about the "coach approach to ministry." Learning how to come alongside the laity and help them uncover their gifts and passions for assisting God to transform the world. It Sounded interesting and like it would be an excellent way to help people find the story they are being called to tell. I was looking forward to it.

This approach to ministry is similar to what we read about in the chapters of the Bible this morning. The relationship of Elijah and Elisha can be seen as one of a "coach approach to ministry." Elijah is walking with Elisha and helping him see God's call. Elisha is also discovering his own uniques set of God-given gifts. It seems as if real ministry and effective ministry can happen when the people of God spend time listening to and communicating with each other to seek God's will.

Be safe. Be warm. Spend time with God.

DAY 27 - THE SIEGE CONTINUES

Today's Reading 2 Kings 4:38 – 2 Kings 15:26

"Yet Jehu was not careful to keep the law of the Lord, the God of Israel, with all his heart. He did not turn away from the sins of Jeroboam, which he had caused Israel to commit."
2 Kings 10:33

Can you imagine what it was like for Cameron Fleming? So what, you don't know who he is? Well, he was a rookie lineman for the New England Patriots. He probably had dreams his whole life to get into the Super Bowl, and his first year, he made it. What an accomplishment!

However, for over a week after the Super Bowl, I am sure he didn't have much celebration happening. He found himself embroiled in "Deflategate." From all media accounts, he is part of the Evil Empire. Every newscast he sees and every newspaper he reads is wall-to-wall coverage of his team and the scandal. I bet he was exhausted listening to the noise.\

Who can blame him, really? You work and train to get to a point all your life, and the memory is tarnished. I thought a lot about Cameron Fleming the days after the Super Bowl and many other nameless and faceless Patriots. The focus was so intense that I almost felt bad for those players, and I can't STAND the Patriots.

Let's be honest for a second, whether the deflating of balls is the Patriots doing or not, people like Cameron Fleming had nothing to do with it. Yet, his reputation could be impacted by whatever is decided. Is it fair? Nope. Is it a reality? Yup. So what do we take from it?

When I read today's reading, I couldn't help but think of the nameless and faceless Israelites. King after King directed the people away from God. We look at that period of Israelite history as a time when the people turned from God. That unfaithfulness becomes their heritage and their legacy. Yet, God's words remind us of something significant.

God held the kings responsible as he did Jehu. Those who lead and teach are called to do so as God leads them. They are called to live lives beyond reproach. They are called to help raise up a generation of people committed to God and changing the world. We are all human, and we all sin. However, more than any other, leaders are called to repent and look not for their own gain but for God's glory to be done.

Maybe Bill Belichick needs to think about the Cameron Flemings of the world a little more. Perhaps we all do.

DAY 28 - TIME MOVES ON.

Today's Reading - 2 Kings 15:27 – 25:30

"Manasseh was twelve years old when he became king, and he reigned in Jerusalem fifty-five years. His mother's name was Hephzibah. He did evil in the eyes of the Lord, following the detestable practices of the nations the Lord had driven out before the Israelites"
2 Kings 21:1-2

We reached the last day of the Bishop's convocation, where we learned about the "coach approach" to ministry. It has been a good time and a very educational one. Understanding the power of presence, deep listening, and powerful questions was an eye-opening thing. These skills are something that can enable me to empower and help people in new ways.

The Israelite Kings needed some excellent coaching. They often found themselves stuck. They needed to be pushed to see how their actions impacted the country, people, and themselves. A good coaching session could help them get unstuck and back to their first love.

If you find yourself stuck today, do a bit of self-coaching. Ask yourself, "what is blocking you from making progress today?" When you spend time discovering what is blocking you, it will be easier to remove those things.

DAY 29 – KEEPING THEM OUT?

Today's Reading 1 Chronicles 1:1 – 9:44

"The gatekeepers: Shallum, Akkub, Talmon, Ahiman and their fellow Levites, Shallum their chief 18 being stationed at the King's Gate on the East, up to the present time. These were the gatekeepers belonging to the camp of the Levites. "
1 Chronicles 9:17

We all know the feeling of waiting in line at the amusement park. Will we make it? Is this the year? What will happen if I can't get on the ride? The waiting can be overwhelming, it seems. Yet, we will all wait; it is a must.

The moment when you finally make it up to the front of the line is when you first see them. They are big and opposing. They seem mean and angry. They are the gatekeepers. They are the ones who make you stand against the sign to see if you are tall enough to make the cut. They are the arbiter if you are allowed to enter.

As we read the chapters this morning, we see gatekeepers being assigned. They are tasked with the protection of the temple. According to what we read this morning, ensuring that all the temple valuables were safe was the central role of these gatekeepers. However, something interesting happens later. By the time we get to 2 Chronicles, the functions of the gatekeepers change. They are now also assigned with keeping the unclean out.

Keeping the unclean out. It seems reasonable...or does it. After all, those gatekeepers in the front of the ride line might not be our friends when we are smaller, but they are tasked with keeping us safe. But how about if their roles expanded. How about choosing who is in or out based on clothing, skin color, age, sex, sexuality, etc. Who are the "deserving" for the ride?

The gatekeepers keeping people away from the God of Abraham just seems wrong. The God of Abraham was a God of freedom and hope. The Israelites desire to give God a home to keep God close had unintended consequences, it seemed. If you can keep God in a box of sorts, perhaps you can decide who gets to visit. Who is worthy. To do that, we need gatekeepers.

The question becomes now, who are the church gatekeepers? Are we still trying to keep the unclean out? Who are the unclean? How many people walk towards the church doors fearful of the looks of the self-appointed gatekeepers?

Are you a gatekeeper? Do you know any gatekeepers? Does God need your protection from the "unclean"?

I think not!

DAY 30 – 33 %
ISN'T PASSING

Today's Reading 1 Chronicles 10:1 – 23:32

"Heman and Jeduthun were responsible for the sounding of the trumpets and cymbals and for the playing of the other instruments for sacred song. The sons of Jeduthun were stationed at the gate."
1 Chronicles 16:42

So we are 1/3 of the way there. It seemed like quite a pipe dream when we started. However, we are 1/3 of the way through our 90-day biblical adventure. Yes, there is reason to be happy, but there is still more reading to do. Hopefully, these 30 days have given us some insight and reignited a powerful connection with the God we read about. I know it has does that for me.

Over these 30 days, if you are like me, there have been days you could not wait to turn the pages and see what God was up to next. On other days, you probably joined me in moaning over-counts and one more round of family lines. Yet, we keep pressing on looking to God for inspiration and guidance. These days have been a journey of power and wonder, and I can't wait to see what God has in store next.

Over the last two days of reading, we have heard mention of the very first Praise and Worship leader, Heman. Heman, along with others, leads the people in praise and makes beautiful music to the Lord. Heman would help those people find a connection with God even when they were less than 100 percent. One thing we have learned in this early reading of the Bible is that worship is vital.

So perhaps you have struggled over the last 30 days finding the time or the excitement needed to read. Maybe you need to look at the next 60 days as a time of worship. Spending time in God's word will be a way for us to experience the glory and wonder of God.

So buckle up...the ride is just beginning.

DAY 31 – MEASURING IT OUT

Today's reading – 1 Chronicles 24:1 – 2 Chronicles 7:10

"Solomon consecrated the middle part of the courtyard in front of the temple of the Lord, and there he offered burnt offerings and the fat of the fellowship offerings, because the bronze altar he had made could not hold the burnt offerings, the grain offerings and the fat portions.I want to accomplish so many things over the next few months."
2 Chronicles 7:7

I have ideas and dreams about what to do. My natural tendency is to simply go day-to-day and do all I can and hope to reach those dreams and visions. The reality is that is not the best way to accomplish anything for me.

Like most people, I must sit down and look at my calendar and resources and really plan. When can I get things done? What can I change? What is within my power? These are essential things for me to wrestle with and strategize over. But, even then, I think it is important to accept my own humanity and understand there might be some problems along the way.

Today's reading takes us into the extensive plans for the temple that Solomon was tasked with building. The materials were gathered, and the workmen were gathered as well. Plans and prayers happened. Eventually, the temple was complete. It seems as if it was spectacular; not one thing was shortchanged. The contractors assigned to the job took no shortcuts.

Yet something happened on opening day. The dedication to the temple was done by Solomon. The people all gathered, and the sacrifices were made. It was then that a slight problem was found. The bronze altar Solomon had made was not big enough to entirely contain the burnt offerings. So he then had to dedicate the middle of the courtyard so that the sacrifices could be made.

Really? After all that planning and all that time, no one noticed a problem was going to happen? Did they simply get caught up in the splendor of the project? Was everyone afraid to tell the king there was a flaw in the plans? It is not apparent in the reading, but something happened.

It is vital to make the plans we need as we move forward. Still, it is also important to remain flexible enough that as situations arise, we can adapt. We need people who are willing to point out upcoming roadblocks and also encourage us along the way when we fall into trouble.

Measure twice....cut once...but be ready to adapt if the cut needs to be reworked.

DAY 32 - THE MAIL IS HERE!

Today's Reading 2 Chronicles 7:11 – 23:15

"Jehoram received a letter from Elijah the prophet"
2 Chronicles 21:12

It doesn't happen as much anymore for you, I am sure, but do you know that feeling when you look into the mailbox, and there is a letter addressed to you? Now, I am not talking about a bill or a jury summons but an actual handwritten letter. So naturally, you get excited because someone has taken the time to sit down and handwrite you a note.

Most people simply send emails, and when we actually mail something, it is still usually produced on word processing software. Most software packages, like Microsoft Word, actually have at least one font that resembles handwriting. This way, you don't even have to take the time to sign your own name; just let the unique font do it for you.

Well, it wasn't always like that. People used to write letters all the time. This was the primary way that people stayed connected to each other. The letter may have had good news and bad news in it. However, those days are pretty much gone. In our reading today, the prophet Elijah sent a letter to King Jehoram. It was not a letter filled with good news.

Jehoram had not been following the ways of God, and was now being reminded of this. God was going to hold him accountable for what he had done. His time as a King would not be an easy one at all. The rest of his reign would be one filled with violence and personal pain. He had strayed too far.

I believe that Jehoram was probably reminded in different ways throughout his life that he needed to follow God and that he had strayed off course. He just did not heed the warnings until it was too late. I believe we have the same things in our lives. We have reminders and warnings when we slip up; we just have to be aware. It might not be a letter or a text, or an email.
However, it might be a person or a situation that happens. We need to keep our eyes open.

Look around today. Take inventory. How are things going? Do you need a do-over? Consider this a letter to you today.

DAY 33 – LOSING IT

Today's Reading 2 Chronicles 23:16 – 35:15

"While they were bringing out the money that had been taken into the temple of the Lord, Hilkiah the priest found the Book of the Law of the Lord that had been given through Moses"
2 Chronicles 34:14

Before the all-powerful GPS that many of us have in our cars or phones, we were slaves to the paper map. Maps showed us the proper routes to take and, more importantly, the ways to avoid. For those in sales or deliveries, we learned the importance of making sure the maps were up to date. You could go nowhere without a map.

Can you imagine how difficult it might have been to find your way around in new areas without those maps or even today without a GPS? It would not be an easy task. I know I would find myself spending a lot of time on the wrong roads or on dead-end streets. We need directions.

So can you imagine the joy of the people when the scroll of instruction was found while rebuilding the temple? The king read the scroll and was reminded just how far off course the people had gone. They had indeed lost their way, and in his hands, he held the proof. This was the key to going back in the right direction.

Reading through the bible, I have been repeatedly reminded of the need to stay connected to God. Reading God's instruction and the depth and the width of God's love is very reassuring. I lived a large part of my life not being concerned with anything that the bible, God, or the church had to say. Life was good, I thought, but now in retrospect, I see how much fuller it could have and should have been.

Are you staying connected? If not, maybe it is time for you to "find" God's word for yourself. You won't be disappointed.

DAY 34 – HELP COMES

Today's Reading 2 Chronicles 35:16 – Ezra 10:44

"This is what Cyrus king of Persia says:
'The Lord, the God of heaven, has given me all the kingdoms of the
earth and he has appointed me to build a temple for him at Jerusa-
lem in Judah. Any of his people among you may go up to Jerusalem
in Judah and build the temple of the Lord, the God of Israel, the God
who is in Jerusalem, and may their God be with them.'"
Ezra 1:2-3

People surprise you sometimes. We often are quick to identify folks into categories. Once they are in these categories, it is easy to identify those categories as "friend," "foe," or "neutral." Foes we can simply dismiss and make no time for. Those we have deemed "neutral," we can take time to figure out if they are friends or foes depending upon what particular thing we are involved in.

Honestly, this process can be very exhausting. Always trying to figure out who fits where. We never seem to understand that there can be another way. We could accept that God is actively at work everywhere. God's grace that goes before us long before we know God is called Prevenient Grace (by United Methodists). The idea is that God is calling to us, wooing us into a relationship.

So if that is true, should we be surprised when people we have identified as enemies come and participate with us in the work of God? Should we be surprised when great things are happening in the world outside the church? I would think we shouldn't be surprised by yet we often are. In fact, we often spend time trying to deny the good of the work being done by people we deem "foe."

In today's reading, we see the reality. God is working in all people. Cyrus, king of Persia, decreed that the rebuilding of the temple would happen. The people of Israel had rebelled against God, and their temple had been destroyed. Many had been in exile. Yet God did not forget them and, in fact, would send a powerful sign. The temple would once again be a beacon to them and a sign that God had not forgotten them.

So perhaps it can be a beacon to us and a reminder that God is at work. Do you trust God? Do you trust that God can work anywhere? If so, let's go see where God is working and go do something!

DAY 35 – YES YOU CAN

Today's Reading Nehemiah 1:1 – 13-14

"Then I prayed to the God of heaven, 5 and I answered the king, 'if it pleases the king and if your servant has found favor in his sight, let him send me to the city in Judah where my ancestors are buried so that I can rebuild it. ' "
Nehemiah 2:4-5

We have all been there. Faced with a significant obstacle or a naysayer. Doubt creeps in, and we start to believe our ability to do the task or task before us. It is human nature to feed into the negative energy that others may place in our way. Negativity is self-feeding after a while. We start believing it and building upon it ourselves.

A couple of weeks ago, I received training in "the coach approach" to ministry. It is a set of tools that helps you in working with people and groups. One of those approaches is to look at a huge problem or issue and think of one thing that YOU can do. In this way, you can begin to make progress, and the considerable problem gets just a bit smaller.

Nehemiah might not have been taught the art of the "coach approach," however he used it very well. He heard reports of the destruction of the walls in Jerusalem. Nehemiah wanted to do something about that overwhelming problem. The one thing he knew to do was pray to God. This was the first step of many that led to the walls rebuilding.

Nehemiah was reassured by God that he could, in fact, undertake this project. He didn't need to be a priest; he could use his upbringing and job skills to navigate the political land mines that he was walking towards. Again, Nehemiah was reassured by God that this could happen.

We all need that kind of reassurance. We need to know that "you can do it." It is important to remember, as Nehemiah did, that God can and will provide that for us. We just need to be in a relationship with God, pray to God, and listen. These things will help us re-build, re-vision, and re-imagine what we can do through the power of God.

Yes, you can...because God can and has.

DAY 36 – BUT WHY SHOULD I?

Today's Reading Nehemiah 13:15 – Job 7:15

"What strength do I have, that I should still hope? What prospects, that I should be patient?"
Job 6:11

Yesterday we looked at the impact that we could have on big things. Today, Job takes us in a different direction entirely. So why should I do anything? Does any of it matter? Job and his buddies seem to be suggesting there is no point in the struggle. So why even bother?

Have you ever felt that way? Struggling with the seeming pointlessness of life can be overwhelming. Terrorism, Racism, Poverty, and unemployment are just a few of the things in the world today that cause fear. What can I really do about them? Is there any point in my efforts at all?

Some of us see perceived unfairness in the world directed towards us and lash out in public forums such as Facebook or Twitter. When I see those posts, I often wonder what folks are trying to accomplish. Do we think that by publicly blaming others, others will jump on board and join in the bashing? If they do, then are we accomplishing anything?

Job is searching and seeking answers to what is going on in his life. He is no longer seeing blessings in his life; instead, he sees cursing in his life. He is beaten down and sees no hope. His friends who happen upon him actually make things worse by heaping more doubt and fear upon him. There is a sense of hopelessness in all that is happening.

Job is wondering what the point is in this thing called life. There is no good ending in his mind so just end it. This fear and hopelessness are almost painful to read. Yet, as I found myself reading it this morning, I just wanted to scream at Job, "Don't give up!".

Hope matters. When you are struggling and don't see a way out, remember God walks with you. God knows you; God loves you. There is hope; life is more than this moment. Keep going. Just keep going. The sun coming up tomorrow brings promises of a new day, new opportunity, and the same powerful hope in God.

Job was never alone...and either are we.

DAY 37 – A WORLD OF GRAY

Today's Reading Job 7:16 – Job 24:25

"Yet I am not silenced by the darkness,
by the thick darkness that covers my face."
Job 23:17

When I worked for IBM, I found a perfectly transactional world. If a computer program did this, then a particular result would happen. I learned that the binary world of computers, in many ways, could make life easy. Simply turn the switch on or off, and you would get the result that you or the client desired. Sure there were problems, but they were merely a matter of looking to see what we had done incorrectly and fixing it.

When I started to go back to church when I was in my 20's, I found in many people a pervasive theology. It was what I call a Sunday School theology. I might have just as quickly named it an IBM theology. The idea behind it being if I do good, then good will happen to me. It is a simple programming mentality. Good code goes in; therefore, good code comes out.

The reading today and the whole book of Job is, in fact, a response to that theology. The world is not simply black and white. Bad things happen to "good" people, and good things happen to "bad" people. We live in a world of gray. A world where things sometimes might not make sense.

So what do we do?

I think what we do is understand that even in a world of gray, we have some clarity. The clarity can be found in God and God's love for us. Whether we have a good day or a bad day, God loves us. So we need to start there. When bad things happen like sickness and disease, understand it is not a punishment from God but a result of sickness and disease in a fallen world. We all will suffer and struggle in life, and in fact, we all will die. This is not God condemning us. It is not even a matter of God being uninvolved; it is the reality of humanity.

At some point, we all will have good things in our life. We will have found treasure and blessings. This is not God saying that we are remarkable above all others. This could be simply another piece of being human. Part of the struggle for us needs to be finding God's grace during the ups and downs of our lives. When we are up, it gives a perfect opportunity to see others in need and help them.

In other words, searching through the gray for God and God's children.

DAY 38 – NAVEL GAZERS R US

Today's Reading Job 25:1 – Job 41:34

"Then the Lord spoke to Job out of the storm."
Job 38:1

You often see it displayed in social media, but social media isn't really the problem. You hear it in conversations, but conversations aren't really the problem either. You listen to it in politicians, but politicians aren't really the problem either. You might even hear it in pastor's sermons, but the sermons aren't really the problem either.

So what is the problem? It is simple really, it is me. At least I can answer for myself. Listen to my rationale for a moment, and perhaps you might agree. I think I can safely say I am the problem because I have done all I can to create a me-centered world, or at least it feels like that at times. I see the world through lenses I have crafted. I evaluate situations through how things impact me.

If not careful, I even may find myself judging God by how quickly a response is given to one of MY needs. The thing is, though, I really don't think I am alone. I am not suffering from this navel-gazing disease alone; it is pervasive in our culture. It seems like it might have started long ago.

After all, read through the book of Job and tell me what you see. We are virtually to the end, and
finally, God is ALLOWED to show up. Job and his cronies have

been so busy telling each other about the God they have crafted in their own minds that they haven't even bothered to go to the source. Instead, they are painting detailed pictures of this God that they think they know. The problem is it is just a limited view of who God truly is.

We can't find God by simply staring at ourselves and our own circumstances. The good news is, though, that we have a God who seeks us out. The God we worship is more significant than any picture we can paint and any image we can see. God is small enough to be in the details and big enough to be beyond the noise.

So perhaps today, I will work on picking my head up and glancing around. I will really strive to see the world and to see the people God has placed before me. I will strive to listen to others and not just hear what I want to hear.

Join me, won't you?

DAY 39 – JUST COMMUNICATE

Today's Reading Job 42:1 – Psalm 24:10

"Why, Lord, do you stand far off?
Why do you hide yourself in times of trouble?"
Psalm 10:1

I have often been fascinated reading through the Psalms, and it appears as if this time will be no different. The psalms are examples of Hebrew poetry and of prayer. But, unfortunately, while I do not doubt this, I think they are also often examples of one other thing…petulant whining.

Now don't run and report me to the nearest Biblical scholar; at least hear me out first. At first glance, you can't help but see it if you are honest. For example, the writer of psalms often calls out for vengeance to be directed towards those that have wronged him. Yet, when the author is not seeking the destruction of enemies many times, he seems to be chastising God for not being around… "WHERE ARE YOU?"

Now don't get me wrong, I am a big fan of the psalms and not simply because I like to whine, although that is part of it! I like the psalms because, at their core, they are some of the most honest prayers you will ever read. There is no pretense. When the prayer is angry, you will know it. When the prayer is sad, you will know that as well. When the prayer praises God, you will encounter some of the deepest and worshipful prayers ever. There is a pure and raw honesty in every line.

Too often, try to find the perfect words or the most clever phrase when praying, especially in public. The psalms are a reminder to me that is not what God wants. What God wants is honesty. What God requires is my heart. If my heart is troubled, then God wants me to share that. If my heart is angry, then God wants me to share that. God wants me to communicate.

So my prayer for myself and for you today is this…I pray that you have the most honest conversation you have had with God in a long time. Don't hold anything back. I know I am about to.

DAY 40 DAYS – STILL LOOKING

Today's Reading Psalm 25:1 – Psalm 45:14
"In you, Lord, I have taken refuge" Psalm 31:1

The Psalms are prayers from people searching. Say these 40 one-word prayers now: Taking a moment and breathing in the word and the image it conveys

Examine
Explore
Hunt
Inquire
Inspect
Investigate
Pursue
Quest
Research
Chase
Search
Prospect
Probe
Sift
Explore
Call
Want
Supplicate
Till
Harvest
Contemplate

Survey
Gaze
View
Discover
Gather
Encounter
Disclose
Uncover
Press
Question
Forward
Speculate
Relate
Commune
Prepare
Unite
Try
Feel
Love

DAY 41 - LOOKING FOR A CONNECTION

Today's Reading Psalm 45:15 – Psalm 69:21

"God is our refuge and strength,
  an ever-present help in trouble.
Therefore we will not fear, though the earth give way
  and the mountains fall into the heart of the sea,
though its waters roar and foam and the mountains quake with their
surging"
Psalm 46: 1-3

 I remembered one night a couple seasons ago, I went to a Philadelphia 76ers preseason game with a friend. It was a good game with flashes of defense and a sporadic night of good offense. However, one moment sticks out above all others. It was a moment when a then 76ers rookie KJ McDaniels had given up his dribble, and then as he hung in the air...well, words can't really adequately describe what I saw. Let's just say he ended up shooting because he had no other choice, all the while contorting his body in physically impossible ways.

It was simply breathtaking. It really was. However, what I remember now about that moment is young KJ. He found himself at that moment isolated and in need of help. THIS TIME he was able to rely on himself and his God-given ability. But what about next time and the time after that? He is playing in a team game and will need a team around him to succeed.

Many of the Psalms I read this morning were reaching out for

God to deliver. The Psalmist realized that he could not do survive on his own. The Psalmist needed a team as well. A team that consists of God and community. We all find ourselves isolated, alone, or lost at times. When that happens, where do you find help?

We are told, our help can be found in God. We are not created to be in isolation; instead, we are made for community. God will help us find that sense of community; all we need do is reach out. Like KJ McDaniels, we can "get the job done on our own" at times. However, we all need saving at times. We all need support.

Where will you find your connection today?

DAY 42 - MORE THAN 42 PIECES

Today's Reading Psalm 69:22 – Psalm 89:13

"You, Lord, showed favor to your land;
 you restored the fortunes of Jacob."
 Psalm 85:1

We have about 100 board games in our house. Some we play often, and others we probably have not played since the kids have been young. Occasionally we will grab a game from the shelf and prepare to play. We have a pattern in our house. I will open the box and familiarize myself with the directions as my wife sets up the board. Every so often, we run into a problem. Something is missing! It might be a die, game piece, or something else.

Sometimes we can work around the problem by borrowing a piece from another game. Every once in a while, however, the missing piece makes the game impossible to play. Our family does not do puzzles often, but the same thing happens when you do a puzzle. The difference is you may not know a puzzle piece is missing until the very end.

Reading today's scriptures reminded me of missing pieces. In Psalm 85, the psalmist asks God to put the people back together...to restore them...to make them whole. The psalmist realizes a missing piece that some of the Israelites might not even have noticed. The missing piece is God.

The Psalmist's prayer is one that perhaps we can pray together today:

> Restore us again, God our Savior.

Will you join me in this prayer today?

DAY 43 - "THANK YOUS" IS NEVER ENOUGH

Today's Reading Psalm 89:14 – Psalm 108:13

"He will call on me, and I will answer him;
I will be with him in trouble,
I will deliver him and honor him."
Psalm 91:15

When our boys were younger, I watched as my wife consistently reminded them to use their manners. For example, she would remind them to say, "please" and "thank you" all the time; I would suggest that perhaps it was a little early to teach those things to the kids. After all, they were too young to remember or understand. But, boy, was I wrong.

So many times when they were growing up, I watched them with pride, fascination, and love as they would be polite and respectful. I never had any doubts or fears that when they were out that they wouldn't act appropriately. Their mother had taught them well.

If only we could extend that in our lives with God and each other all the time. Too often, those manners we had picked up when we were younger are forgotten. We begin to believe that we are the source of all the good that happens and that others, and even God, are the reasons things don't go our way. We need a refresher course.

The readings this morning were just that for me. A reminder that through my "ups and downs," that God has remained faithful. Even when I have turned away, consciously or unconsciously, God has stayed by my side. Sometimes I forget that.

I look at my calendar and everything I have to accomplish and wonder how I will get it done. I speak about good things that happen in my life, and I am quick to claim the credit. I see the stumbles andI am quick to lay blame at all the people who I believe have gotten in the way.

Today will be different. Today, I will strive to be grateful. I will find ways to thank those who have done so much and walked alongside me. Finally, I will take the time to thank God for it all. I start now. For those of you who have been reading these last 43 days...thank you. For those who have reached out, thank you. Your support means a lot.

Thank you, God, for waking me up and focusing me each morning.

Thanks!

DAY 44 - 44 FOR ME AND 1 FOR YOU

Today's Reading Psalm 109:1 – Psalm 134:3

"The Lord is gracious and righteous;
*   our God is full of compassion.*
The Lord protects the unwary;
*   when I was brought low, he saved me."*
Psalm 115: 5-6

I can still remember. It has been decades, but in many ways, it seems like just yesterday. I remember what turned out to be my only fight in grade school. We were just young dumb kids. I was tired of him messing around with me all the time. It seemed day after day, he would pick on me. I just let it go and added it up. This day, however, was different.

I couldn't take one more perceived slight, and I did not. I am not sure what the "indignity" I suffered that day at school, but it was the last one. I dropped my book-bag in the schoolyard, and we were fighting. Now I am not sure how much fighting actually happened. Even then, I was not a big fan of getting punched in the face. So I did a lot of bobbing and weaving. Finally, I was just determined to make him pay.

All these years later and two things stick out to me about that circumstance. Number one, how silly that was. Number two, how glad I am that God does not keep tally like I did and still do at times. If God was ticking off all the ways that I have failed or disobeyed, then I would be in big trouble. If God was as vengeful as I want to be at times, then mine would have been a short, painful, and miserable existence.

Instead of giving me what I deserve, we have a God who gives us grace that we could never earn. We are not lorded over by a task-master but instead loved by the creator. So maybe my prayer for us today is simply one of peace. A peace that comes from letting go of scorekeeping and letting go of built-up hostility. I pray instead for God to guide us today and focus us not on other's misdeeds but instead on the blessings we have been given. Sounds like a plan to me.

DAY 45 - TIME FOR A MIDTERM

Today's Reading Psalm 135:1 – Proverbs 6:35

"Then you will understand what is right and just
    and fair—every good path.
For wisdom will enter your heart,
    and knowledge will be pleasant to your soul.
Discretion will protect you,
    and understanding will guard you."
Proverbs 2: 9-11

Midterms were never fun for me. I remember when I had my first midterms in high school. I was not sure of the procedure. In school, I was used to being tested on just a particular section or chapter. Suddenly, I was now required to remember things we had talked about when the class started months ago. It didn't seem fair.

Every once in a while, we would have one of those teachers who thought as I thought. The midterm would only consist of what we had gone over since the previous test. So just another test, but usually one that was worth more to my overall grade. I could deal with that. If only life could be like that.

The thing is, though, life isn't like that. Life is really about all we have learned and how we are using it. Our time through the bible over the last 45 days is really no different. What have we learned? How will we use it? These really are vital questions for me today. So let's get ready for a midterm.

A few years ago, the late Bishop Reuben Job wrote a tiny but powerful book, Three Simple Rules, A Wesleyan Way of Living. The book was Job's take on John Wesley's General Rules. They were simple, but they were powerful. As we look over the last 45 days and prepare for our midterm, we see them throughout scripture and today's reading.

"Do no harm."

It is a simple rule, really. However, throughout the readings we have had, we see evidence of it not being followed. Adam and Eve ate the forbidden fruit. Cain killing his brother Abel. Joseph's brothers sold him into slavery. These are examples of those who did harm. The bible is filled with examples.

We are called to do no harm as well. Don't lie, cheat, or steal. Do not injure or harm our brothers and sisters. Avoid the many "-isms" that are prevalent in the world today. Do not ignore those in need. Do not oppress or overburden others.

"Do good"

Do good. Does it get any easier than that? It seems like it should be a simple thing. However, in the bible and in our lives, we know that is not always the case. In the bible, we see plenty of examples though of people doing good. We see Joseph avoiding Potipher's wife. We read about Hannah praying for and dedicating her son to God. We read about Queen Esther standing up for her people.

We are called to do good as well. This does not have to be big sweeping gestures, although it could be. Helping those in need. Providing kindness to those who you see. Teaching, assisting, loving, caring. These are simple ways to do good each and every day.

"Stay in love with God."

As we prepare for our midterm, the last rule we need to know is this plea to stay in love with God. Again, it seems easy enough but is it really? We see evidence in scripture that this is something that the Israelite people continued to struggle within their lives. They would often forget their first love. They would turn away.

Staying in love with God means knowing God. Knowing God means being in a relationship with God. Doing that means we need to read scripture, worship, and pray. This is how we stay connected. This is how we stay in love.

Okay, are you ready for the midterm? The good news is that it is an open-book test. In fact, it is an open heart and open mind test as well!

DAY 46 - WISDOM, HOMER SIMPSON, AND DONUTS... MMM DONUTS!

Today's Reading Proverbs 7:1 – 20:21

*"The one who gets wisdom loves life;
the one who cherishes understanding will soon prosper."*
Proverbs 19:8

It is always a good thing to see a character in a television show or movie that we can make fun of because of the ridiculous things that they do. In that character, we can often place ourselves and think of how to handle a situation better. We find joy in the misfortune of that character because we believe those things would never happen to us.

For me, it helps me suspend disbelief even more, when it is a cartoon character. There is no way that I could ever find myself in the silly situations that these crazy cartoon characters find themselves. At least, that is the rationale that I use when I watch some of these shows from time to time. But, unfortunately, the truth is often just a little different.

When we really look at some of these cartoons, we see people simply trying the best they can to do the best they can. The absurdity of the situations notwithstanding, I think we all can relate to that. I think when we watch Homer Simpson, Peter Griffin, or Bob Belcher, we can understand their passion, however misguided it often turns out. We all are trying to make it. We all are looking for wisdom.

Today's readings help us to see that this is not a new situation. People have been searching for wisdom, knowledge, and truth since the beginning of time. The problem becomes when we look in the wrong places and focus on the wrong things. The disaster happens when we are distracted by Jimmy Pesto, a giant fighting chicken, donuts (mmmm donuts), or whatever distracts us from finding real wisdom, knowledge, and truth.

The Proverbs help to remind us that these things are found with God. God is our strong tower; God is our refuge. Godly wisdom is a gift. So can we focus our attention on God...seek God's counsel...pray for God's wisdom...in the midst of all that the world has to distract us?

My prayer for you today:
God, we seek you first. Help us. Show us. Lead us. Amen

DAY 47 - LITTLE THINGS MATTER

Today's Reading Proverbs 20:22 – Ecclesiastes 2:26

"Eat honey, my son, for it is good;
honey from the comb is sweet to your taste.
Know also that wisdom is like honey for you:
If you find it, there is a future hope for you,
and your hope will not be cut off."
Proverbs 24: 13-14

One morning I walked outside to start the car, and it just would not cooperate. It was too cold for my car to kick over. If I could not get the car started and moved out of the way, I was unsure how my wife would get to work. I tried it once, no go. I tried it the second time, and it almost started. Finally, on the third attempt, it started. Success!

It was a small thing in reality, but for me, on that particular morning, it was huge. The car starting enabled the rest of my day to continue as planned and for us to not have to panic and worry about what to do next. Sometimes we take those little things for granted. The alarm waking us up in the morning. The Keurig working in the morning. The car starting. The Wifi working.

Each of these things on there own are tiny and straightforward things. However, in my life, these are essential things. Something I was reminded of this morning. Part of today's reading touched on the little things. It reminded me of how God often uses things that society does not value or does not value as God does.

Throughout the Old Testament, we are reminded of this as God uses the youngest son to lead the people. We are reminded of it throughout the story of Esther as God uses a woman to bring freedom and safety to the people. God's story of using those on the margin continues throughout scripture. The biblical story reminds us that all life matters. God values each of us.

That morning was a reminder to me that I need to be more aware and thankful. I need to keep my eyes open and keep mindful of the little and big things that happen around me. Excuse me, I have to go. My coffee just finished brewing!

DAY 48 - THAT'S THE POINT, AFTER ALL.

Today's Reading Ecclesiastes 3:1 – Song of Songs 8:14

"There is a time for everything,
 and a season for every activity under the heavens"
Ecclesiastes 3:1

Some days you look at the day ahead and wonder what the point is. It seems pointless. I think this is probably true no matter what you do in your life. When I was in school, there were some classes that I just didn't see the point of what I was doing and why I was doing it. Some days at work, as I got older, there seemed to be no point. Another day and perhaps 50 more pizzas delivered. Another day and a couple dozen more lines of computer code. What is the point?

When I read the book of Ecclesiastes, I understand the seeming hopelessness that permeates the writing. I really do. We have all been there at times. However, I find it incredible that right after the book of Ecclesiastes, we see the Song of Songs. We go from hopelessness to overflowing hope. We go from despair to excitement. We go from questions to answers found in relationship.

After all, isn't that what life is at times? Ebbs and flows are part of what we feel and experience. However, we yearn for a relationship. We find comfort and purpose in relationship to each other and to God. The point of the struggle is often struggling WITH others. I read the words in today's scripture, and I see hope and promise. I know the power of belonging and the promise of tomorrow.

Today, the point seems clear. God loves us and calls us to be in relationship with each other. So don't let doubt and despair overwhelm you.
The point is…relationship.

DAY 49 - WHAT NUMBER MATTERS?

Today's Reading Isaiah 1:1 – Isaiah 13:22

"People will oppress each other—
man against man, neighbor against neighbor.
The young will rise up against the old,
the nobody against the honored."
Isaiah 2: 5

Today, I wake up with a few things still to do. I need to burn the palms and finish up my worship plan for this evening. I also need to ensure that tonight follows the overall theme we are doing for Lent. In addition to that, I have several phone calls I need to make and a few emails to return. Nothing overwhelming but a typical fun-filled day.

We begin our journey through Lent today, and depending on how you count, it is either a 40 or 46-day journey. In some ways, it is all about semantics, and other days, it speaks to the meaning of Lent itself. However, as I was doing math this morning, I came upon a number that speaks to Lent and today's readings more than any other. Back to that number in a bit.

Today's reading in Isaiah was a challenge. It was God's word to a group of people who have turned away from God. It was about God's people playing AT religion and missing the point of it all. God didn't want their sacrifices; he despised them. God wanted their hearts. God told them the way to God's heart was what they ignored; the widow and the orphan, The people of Israel, ignored the marginalized and the oppressed. God was not happy.

Would God be any happier with us today? Let's go back to that number. The number is not 40 or 46 but 552. According to Courier-Post article several years ago , 552 was the approximate number of homeless people here in Gloucester County. 552 is a tragedy. 552 is an outrage. 552 is a number that hurts the very heart of God. 552 could very well be a low number.

Every year there is a meme that goes around about 40 things to give up for Lent. It is a great idea, and I support the idea. However, for me, it isn't enough. If, in fact, Lent is a time for us to turn back to God...I need to do more. So I invite you to join me where you are or participate with me here.

Here in Gloucester County, many places help the homeless and poor. I encourage you to do one of the following:

Have your church or club, or office
Collect 552 cans for the local food bank.
Collect 552 dollars for a local program that deals with Homeless families.
Collect 552 books for the local school library to help children engage in education.

What matters? People matter.

DAY 50 - THERE IS TIME, RIGHT?

Today's Reading Isaiah 14:1 – Isaiah 28:29

"In that day the people who live on this coast will say, 'See what has happened to those we relied on, those we fled to for help and deliverance from the king of Assyria!
How then can we escape?'"
Isaiah 20:6

Resolutions are seemingly part of life:
"I resolve to get in shape."
"I resolve to eat better."
"I resolve to pray more."
"I resolve to be a better dad."
"I resolve to be a better husband."
"I resolve to be a better friend."
"I resolve to be a better disciple."

These are some of the resolutions that have passed my lips in days, weeks, and months passed. Every single one of these I meant when I said it. I tried to honor those resolutions. Unfortunately, in many cases, I failed time and time again. Failure seems inevitable in many ways.

However, what I have noticed is that over time the feeling of failure dissipates. There will always be a tomorrow. There will always be time to get fit. There will always be time to be better. There will always be time to get right. Until there isn't.

The words in Isaiah today speak to a people who were lost. Many of them lost forever. They had made decisions that had directed their days. Many of those decisions were counter to God's design. The people suffered the repercussions of those choices. I believe many of those people, at some point, probably made their own resolutions. However, like many of us, they probably thought there was time to get back on track. Until there wasn't.

Today can be a time of change. A time of repentance. A time of new beginnings. The thing is, change, repentance, and new beginnings need to start at some point. There won't always be a tomorrow.

So let's start today.

DAY 51 – BACK TO THE BASICS

Today's Reading Isaiah 29:1 – Isaiah 41:18

"Lord Almighty, the God of Israel, enthroned between the cherubim, you alone are God over all the kingdoms of the earth. You have made heaven and earth. Give ear, Lord, and hear; open your eyes, Lord, and see; listen to all the words Sennacherib has sent to ridicule the living God."
Isaiah 37: 16-17

When my children were younger, it seemed like a large portion of our time together was my wife and me answering one question after another.

"Why?"
"How come?"
"When?"
"How?"

We were faced with one question after another. Never earth-shattering, at least to us. Yet, the questions and the need for answers seemed almost life-altering at times for our kids. There were times that I wanted just a moment of peace from the process. But, looking back now, I think of the whole thing differently.

Our children wanted to be with us. They wanted to share time with us. They wanted to hear our voice. They just wanted to be near us. It was all about being together. It was a time they learned to trust us with their fears and doubts, and questions. It was a time when they could just learn to be themselves with us.

In many ways, that is what our prayer life should be with God. Asking questions, sharing our fears, and dreaming together with God. Two different times in today's reading, we read about the prayers of King Hezekiah. These are the prayers of a man comfortable from being with God.

They are prayers of fear and hope.
What I read when I see these prayers is a child asking those same questions my kids asked us:

"Why?"
"How come?"
"When?"
"How?"

Do you trust God enough to pray these prayers today? Will you share your fears with God? When is the last time you spent time with God in prayer? Take time today to share your life with God.

My prayer for us today:
Lord,
You are everything to us. So today, listen to my fears. Hear my dreams. Share time with me.
Amen.

DAY 52 - NO WORRIES

Today's Reading Isaiah 41:19 – Isaiah 52:12

But you will not leave in haste
  or go in flight;
for the Lord will go before you,
  the God of Israel will be your rear guard.
Isaiah 52:12

In the military, you learn a lot of different skills. You are taught about the meaning of respect. You are taught about responsibility. You are shown how to accomplish things that you never believe you would be able to do. However, there is one lesson even more important than all of these things.

Above all else, you learn the value of depending on each other. You are taught the importance of teamwork. This lesson is drilled into you over and over again. When the individual fails, the team fails. When the individual succeeds, it is a team victory. It is a great feeling knowing that no matter what happens, someone always has your back.

A few year ago, there was an educational push in our country called "Got your 6". This was terminology that was sprinkled into television shows and into our general everyday life. The idea was for the government to connect to the military that we had coming back from Iraq and Afghanistan, and other places. We were being conditioned to remember that we needed to support these men and women as they came back.

"Got your 6" was a World War 1 term used by fighter pilots. It was something that would be said to reference the back of the planes. So the pilots would know that someone was looking out for them when they couldn't see all the lurking danger. So for us to be able to say "Got your 6" to veterans as they come home is a powerful statement. They are not alone.

Today's reading reminded us that someone has got our back as well. God is described as our rearguard. No matter where we go and what we find ourselves dealing with, God is there with us. We are never in isolation because of God. This comfort is ours for the taking. We can boldly go into the world and do those things God directs us because God has "got our 6".

What have you been worrying about? What have you been fearful of? What has overwhelmed you?

No worries. God is here.

DAY 53

Today's Reading Isaiah 52:13 - Isaiah 66:18

"Come, all you who are thirsty,
*   come to the waters;*
and you who have no money,
*   come, buy and eat!*
Come, buy wine and milk
*   without money and without cost"*
Isaiah 55:1

Some days I have the need to be welcomed in and today is one of those days. Have you ever struggled with feeling as if you are enough? It is not a good feeling, but it is not unusual. We all go through those periods of time whether we want to admit it out-laid or not. These words from the prophet today were just what I needed.

It is an invitation without reservation. I am not expected to provide anything. Just me and that is an incredible reality. God wants me. Yet, I have some more good news. This invitation is not just for me. It is for you and for the guy down the street. Yeah, that guy. The one who bugs you. See that is the thing. This invitation is for everyone. God wants us all. God is a God of love and community. Community can be messy, but there is nothing better.

So come on in. You are welcome here.

DAY 54 – DISTRACTIONS ARE GONNA GET YA!

Today's Reading Isaiah 66:19 – Jeremiah 10:13

"My people have committed two sins:
They have forsaken me,
    the spring of living water,
and have dug their own cisterns,
    broken cisterns that cannot hold water."
Jeremiah 2:13

I often tease my wife when she forgets what she is doing or what she is saying by suggesting she was distracted by "a pretty butterfly." We often kid around about it, but the reality is, we all have butterflies that we are distracted by throughout the day. So the question for us becomes, can we identify and deal with those butterflies.

For me, it is often breaking sports news. I am intrigued by whatever the "talking heads" are talking about at any given moment. It is not unusual for me to tune them in and tune out the rest of the world for way too long. I have had to make changes in my daily routine to ensure these distractions aren't too time-consuming.

The distractions in my life have not been life-threatening, and I do not think that they will be. However, those butterflies can become all-consuming and very dangerous. There can come a time when we lose track of time and surroundings and put ourselves and others in danger. This could come from things as innocuous as cell phones or as potentially troublesome as alcohol.

Today's scripture readings point us to the ultimate danger of distraction. God's words to the prophet Jeremiah are words of lament and warning. The people have lost their way. They have been distracted by focusing on the accomplishments that they feel come from their own hands. They are consumed with looking for other gods in many different places. Their distractions have caused them to neglect God.

What can we do? How can we enjoy life and still remain close to God? Enjoy those butterflies but remember and worship not the butterfly but the Creator. Thanks to God for the butterflies in our lives, but don't let them take over our lives. Ultimately every butterfly, every rainbow, and every blessing is from God. So let's spend more time focused on the creator and less time on the creation.

DAY 55 - SAMMY HAGAR IS SINGING THE SOUNDTRACK OF OUR LIVES.

Today's Reading Jeremiah 10:14 – Jeremiah 23:8

"But they did not listen or pay attention; instead, they followed the stubbornness of their evil hearts. So I brought on them all the curses of the covenant I had commanded them to follow but that they did not keep."
Jeremiah 11:8

"One foot on the brake and one on the gas, hey
 Well, there's too much traffic, I can't pass, no
 So I tried my best illegal move
 A big black and white come and crushed my groove again"

Growing up, these lyrics were ingrained in me. Sammy Hagar was singing for ME. He had my thoughts and my desires, and he put them over the radio waves for me. This song spoke not only for me but to me. I didn't want to be confined by rules and limits. I was a man. I was free. I was independent.

"Write me up for 125
 Post my face, wanted dead or alive
 Take my license, all that jive
 I can't drive 55, oh yeah"

Even now, reading these lyrics and singing the song once again in my head, I almost feel a pang for the old days. No commitment, no fear, no worry, and no concerns. Or perhaps that feeling is heartburn from last night's dinner? See, that makes more sense, especially in light of today's readings.

Reading through Jeremiah this morning was a reminder. A reminder that there are repercussions for decisions that we make. There are consequences, and sometimes they can be severe. Sammy Hagar spoke to a generation that thought they were being ignored and stifled by the world. Jeremiah is the instrument that God chooses to talk to a world about God being ignored.

Jeremiah's words remind us that we are not lone wolves. We are part of a larger community. Everyone matters, and everyone is impacted by our decisions. When we ignore those in need, God notices. When we turn our backs on those on the margins, God weeps. When we worship the gods of money, power, and prestige, God sees that and gets angry.

So on this 55th day of reading (see what I did there), we are reminded that we are not alone. God is holding us accountable. We are strongest when we are faithful to God and connected to our brothers and sisters.

Do you value freedom more than people? Do you value independence more than the "other"?

What is God saying to you this morning?

DAY 56 - WHAT DOES HOPE LOOK LIKE?

Today's Reading Jeremiah 23:9 – Jeremiah 33:22

"I knew that this was the word of the Lord; 9 so I bought the field at Anathoth from my cousin Hanamel and weighed out for him seventeen shekels of silver."
Jeremiah 32:9

Several years ago, I read "Long Walk to Freedom," the autobiography of Nelson Mandela. It was an incredible tale of perseverance against daunting obstacles. The more I read, the more I became shocked at how people treat each other for many different reasons. But, also, the more I read, the more I felt filled with hope. Despite how we often treat each other, the human spirit is an incredible thing.

For me, the book told a tale of just what power is contained within love, hope, and faith. If you love, you feel as if anything is possible. If you have hope, you know better days are ahead. If you have faith in something, you take that love and hope into action. Nelson Mandela helped to lead his people and the world into a brighter future in many ways.

Today's reading takes us to people in need of hope. They are a people in turmoil and a people being displaced. All around them, there is trouble. All around them is fear. Amid that fear, Jeremiah buys some land. This land becomes a symbol of future hope. It is a symbol of love. It is an act of faith. God has led Jeremiah to this point. Jeremiah trusts in God.

Do you trust God with your future? Even in the darkest hour, do you have hope? Does your faith in God propel you into action? If not...why not?

DAY 57 - I KNOW...
I REALLY DO

Today's Reading Jeremiah 33:23 – Jeremiah 47:7

"Whenever Jehudi had read three or four columns of the scroll, the king cut them off with a scribe's knife and threw them into the firepot, until the entire scroll was burned in the fire." Jeremiah 36:23

Before you read any further, I want you to know that I am the most intelligent person I know. I am not trying to brag, and I am not trying to be obnoxious. I am simply trying to state the facts as I see them. It is a public service of sorts. It is the only thing that makes sense after all.

How else can I explain it? It can only be attributed to my intelligence. What is "it," you ask? Well, "it" is my apparent lack of trusting what people said before I went off and did my own thing anyway. "It" is my disregard for excellent advice because I know a better way. "It" is my stubbornness in asking for advice or actually following the advice when given.

I suppose there is another way to look at "it." I can define "it" as sin. In today's reading, Jeremiah tells the people the word from the Lord, and consistently the people do not listen. The people ask for the word from the Lord, and when Jeremiah tells them, they do not listen. They see what has happened all around them and still...THEY DO NOT LISTEN.

I struggle. I really do; I struggle with this thing called pride. I get caught up in what I think I know or how I know better. I find myself drifting from time to time away from where God is leading. I need centering. I need to be anchored in the word. This time of reflecting on reading God's word is helping me do just that.

It is helping me make this time a priority in my life. I want to listen. I want to hear. I want to listen.
How about you?

DAY 58 - WHAT'S OUT THERE?

Today's Reading Jeremiah 48:1 – Lamentations 1:22

"Then the city wall was broken through, and the whole army fled. They left the city at night through the gate between the two walls near the king's garden, though the Babylonians[a] were surrounding the city"
Jeremiah 52:7

Several years ago, my wife and I and our youngest son joined other colleagues and their families and made the trek to Israel. It was the first time that I had ever been there, and it was a great experience. The people and land that I had read about and been taught about since I was a child were right before me. It was, at times, overwhelming.

Two things struck me immediately as we began to tour the land. The first was just how compact everything was. When I had read the biblical accounts prior, in my head, there was an idea that this was a vast land. The distance in my head between Bethlehem and Jerusalem was enormous. I learned that geographically that was not the case; however, for the story of Jesus, they still represent a great distance, the beginning, and the end.

The second thing that struck me was the checkpoint system. For those that do not know, there are a series of crossings and checkpoints throughout Israel. They exist to control and monitor the passing of goods and people, particularly Palestinians, throughout the region. It was a jarring thing for me to see and to witness. Even years later, several of our encounters at check-points remain burned into my memory.

Our tour guide was a wonderful man with a Palestinian heritage. He shared with us the impact of the story of Jesus from his own context in ways that I had never heard before. He was a brother in Christ. His passion was so evident. Yet, he was forced to leave certain city areas by a particular time and had to leave us early several days. It was again a jarring reminder of fences, walls, and barricades.

Today's readings spoke about the walls of Jerusalem as the army of Babylon surrounded it, preparing to invade Jerusalem. I can only imagine the fear of the people trapped inside the walls as they were made aware of the invaders. The tension was probably rising daily. Even reading the passages, the feeling of trouble rang from the pages(of my kindle).

See that is the thing about walls, fences, and barricades. We often set them up to keep people out, but they always keep us locked in. As a result, we separate ourselves from each other and live in fear of each other and the unknown. The walls, fences, and barriers make prisoners of us all.

It goes without saying that these barriers we create don't always have to be physical. We try to hide away from others from fear or to protect ourselves, or even from shame. We struggle to connect with God because being in a relationship with God creates change in us. The walls are a response to our fear of that change.

What are you trying to keep out? What are you trying to lock in? Where is God trying to break down your walls?

DAY 59 - WHAT FEEDS YOU?

Today's Reading Lamentations 2:1 – Ezekiel 12:20

"And he said to me, 'Son of man, eat what is before you, eat this scroll; then go and speak to the people of Israel.' So I opened my mouth, and he gave me the scroll to eat. "
Ezekiel 3:1

I was up a little early for a Saturday morning. I had a busy day ahead of me, and we decided to start the day off with a trip to the gym. Unfortunately, the weather had not been very cooperative in allowing us to walk outside. In addition, this old body needed some major tuning up. So off to the gym we were going.

In preparation for us going back to the gym, I had to be more aware of what I was buying at the grocery store yesterday as I was food shopping. Nothing major, but more apples and fewer Oreos! It was a sad trip pushing the cart past Oreos, Chips Ahoy, and Nutter Butters. However, in the end, I realize it would be counterproductive to feed my body an excess of junk if I was going to the gym to try to get fit.

I think we all understand that process. Sometimes we follow it, but sometimes we don't. I think the struggle is with what ELSE we are feeding ourselves. In today's reading, there is power imagery during Ezekiel's prophesy. The one thing that stuck with me is Ezekiel being told to eat the scroll containing the word of God. It was a strong reminder for me.

We need to spend a lot of time with God, not just try to fit God in on Sundays or as we are falling asleep. Read the Bible, Pray, Fellowship, Worship, and Serve are all ways we can do just that. Look at that list again. How long has it been since you have done one of those things? What can you do today to change that? Who can hold you accountable? What will that look like once you get it done?

What is feeding you today?

DAY 60 - STOP IT

Today's Reading Ezekiel 12:21 – Ezekiel 23:39

 "But if a righteous person turns from their righteousness and commits sin and does the same detestable things the wicked person does, will they live? "
Ezekiel 18:24

I have a friend who tells of a story of a 10-speed bike and a Christmas long ago. He wanted a 10-speed bicycle. All his friends had 10-speed bikes, but not just any 10-speed bike; he wanted a Schwinn. It was the bike all his friends had or were going to get. So, my friend covered all the bases. He told Santa about the bike. He told his parents about the bike. He told his grandparents about the bike. Everyone knew.

On Christmas Eve that year, his parents woke him up and told him the good news...Santa had come! He followed them up the stairs with great excitement. He went into the bathroom, where he apparently left his present. He went in, and there it was, a brand new red 10-speed bike. It was great. It was precisely what he wanted. Until he looked closer. It was then he found to his horror, it was not a Schwinn at all. It was from Kmart. He was devastated.

He was a bright boy and did all he could to hide his disappointment. Santa tried, and his parents were great, but he wasn't entirely filled with Christmas joy. As he rode his new bike on Christmas morning, he felt as if everyone was watching him rise his "not a Schwinn." As he ran into other friends those days, he couldn't help notice their new rides were mostly Schwinns. He never got over it, and all the days and years he had that bike, those feelings never wholly left him.

I thought of that story this morning as I was reading the scripture passages. The people of Israel heard a powerful word. They were favored by God, and despite that, they wanted more. They looked around and felt that God had provided out of love was not enough; they deserved more. It made me angry reading it today. I began to judge the Israelites as God was, and then I remembered the bike.

How many times do we ignore or downplay our own life and want what someone else has? How often do we look at the world and see something good happen to someone and think we deserve that and not the other person? So today's reading for me was a reminder to be thankful. It was a wake-up call of sorts. Stop being bratty. Stop being greedy. Stop always wanting.

Just...stop it.

What is God saying to you?

DAY 61 - EVERY BIT OF IT

Today's Reading Ezekiel 23:40 – Ezekiel 35:15

" *For this is what the Sovereign Lord says: 'I myself will search for my sheep and look after them. As a shepherd looks after his scattered flock when he is with them, so will I look after my sheep. I will rescue them from all the places where they were scattered on a day of clouds and darkness.'* "
Ezekiel 34: 11-12

I struggle with math; I really do. I am good at the memorization part of math. I was taught multiplication tables as a youth and still can recite them. I can do simple math in my head and very well. It is the concepts that get me through. Rules and laws and the like are impossible for me. I am not sure why but it is just something I have been inept dealing with.

However, I do believe that we often make math way more difficult than we need to. Perhaps it happens because some people want to feel smart. It might happen because we wish to have a more nuanced argument. I am sure there are a lot of reasons; however, none of them seem valid to me. The truth is we just like to make things more complex at times.

For instance, there is an elementary math lesson in today's scripture reading. You could think of it as a pie chart of sorts. God lets the people know exactly how much he cares and how much the world is accountable to God. So let's look at the pie chart now:

The whole thing...every bit of it...God's. Not a sliver, not the crust; God wants and cares for the entire thing. 100 percent of the pie and people belong to God. It sounds pretty simple, yet we struggle with it. We try to create scenarios where some of what we see is secular and other is holy. Yet, this is not the image of God we see in the Bible. God is holding all the people accountable. God loves all the people and often waits for them to accept and love and obey.

The critical math here is God cares about you from the tip of your head to the bottom of your toes. God wants what is best for you. 100 percent of your concerns, God wants to share. God also feels the same about the noisy neighbor you have. In fact, that cousin, you know the one, God cares about her as well.

In God's math, the only math that counts, we all matter.
Yup, even me.

DAY 62 - JUST WHAT I NEEDED

Today's Reading Ezekiel 36:1 – Ezekiel 47:12

"The man brought me back to the entrance to the temple, and I saw water coming out from under the threshold of the temple toward the east (for the temple faced east)"
Ezekiel 47:1

One morning I was heading out the door a little earlier than I usually was out and about. However, I was on my way to a conference gathering with other clergy. I woke up early to make a few green smoothies for my wife and me for the day. A little health jump-start for us as we continue to try to get and stay healthy and fit. A green smoothie is not what I felt as if I needed that morning in reality.

What I felt as if I needed was a bottomless cup of coffee. You know the ones I mean. You slide into a booth, and the waitress who has been working there for decades says, "Coffee?". There would be very few things that would sound so good. The pot she would bring over would be fresh and hot and remain so for each cup I drink. What a feeling that would be.

Perhaps this is much like Ezekiel's feeling as he sees in a vision of the River of Healing in the scripture passage today. He sees an endless supply of water that starts as a trickle but deepens and widens as it goes. He is told that this water restores and provides life. What a feeling that must have been for him. He saw the source of the river, the Temple, and knew God was there.

Whatever you want to call it, the river of life, living water, or abundant life, God provides it. The God Ezekiel knows and that we know will continue to provide for the people. So our role is to get into the river, taste the living water, accept the abundant life, and enjoy.

Are you enjoying the life God has provided? Are you able to feel the healing of the river and the life in the water? Is it changing you?

DAY 63 - COURAGE

Today's Reading Ezekiel 47:13 – Daniel 8:27

So the king gave the order, and they brought Daniel and threw him into the lions 'den. The king said to Daniel, "May your God, whom you serve continually, rescue you!"
Daniel 6:16

Growing up, one of my highlights each year was the night in which the Wizard of Oz would be on television. It was an exciting time. I couldn't wait to see Dorothy, Scarecrow, and the Tin Man; each year, it brought excitement, fear, and thrills. However, one character made it a must-watch television for me; the Cowardly Lion.

He was amusing and, at the same time, very depressing. The Cowardly Lion had big plans and great intentions but let the fear get the best of him. The Cowardly Lion knew how to act brave, well, at least part of the time. Yet, everyone watching realized very quickly it was all just a show. Faced with danger, the Cowardly Lion reverts back to form repeatedly throughout the movie.

In today's readings, we see what real courage looks like and where it comes from. Daniel is faced with a problem. The King has been tricked into signing a law that Daniel will not follow because of his relationship with God. God alone is worthy of worship. Daniel is trapped by the law. The result is that instead of dishonoring God, he is thrown in a den with Lions.

Daniel had a choice.
You have a choice.

I have a choice.

The choice is whether we will allow the pressure from the world, in whatever forms they come, to force us from turning away from our relationship with God. Real courage is found in obedience to God. Real courage is found in our relationship with God. We know that nothing can impact us or triumph over us when we walk with God.

The Cowardly Lion received a medal of courage from the Wizard of Oz in the movie. It is an outward sign of what is internalized in the Cowardly Lion and has been there the whole time. It is a sacramental moment in the movie.

The Lion chose to stand up and do the right thing in the movie. Daniel stood up to do the right thing as well. What about you?

What is God asking you to stand up to, or who is God asking you to stand up for today?

DAY 64 – PICK ONE ALREADY

Today's Reading Daniel 9:1 – Hosea 13:6

"Hear the word of the Lord, you Israelites,
because the Lord has a charge to bring
against you who live in the land:
There is no faithfulness, no love,
no acknowledgment of God in the land."
Hosea 4:1

In second grade, I had the biggest crush on a girl in my class. I liked everything about her. I enjoyed spending time with her. I liked how she looked. I liked how she talked. I just didn't know if she liked me back. So I devised a plan. It was a good plan; some would call it foolproof.

I wrote her a note. The note was similar to the picture above. I asked three simple questions: Do you like me? Yes. No. Maybe. Circle One. It was brilliant. It couldn't fail. I worked up my courage and handed her the note. I waited confidently for her response. 4 decades later, and I still haven't heard back on the note! Ultimately, it worked out perfectly for us both. So I am glad my note didn't have the effect I had intended it to.

I do remember that waiting, though. It was a time of in-between, where I used to be and where I was going to be. There was not much I could do during that time of waiting, though. All I could continue to do was be the goofy 2nd grader I had always been and hope that was good enough for her.

In today's reading, we see God responding to God's desire. God loves us. God wants us. God desires to be in a relationship with us. Yet, just like the people of Israel, we have treated God poorly, like a disposable lover. We seemingly have kept God around for the good stuff but don't want to be tied down if something better comes along.

What is it going to take for us to go all-in with God? What will it take us to leave behind all those things that keep us from God? God is waiting for us. God loves us.

What are you waiting for?

DAY 65 - WHAT WOULD HAPPEN?

Today's Reading Hosea 13:7 – Amos 9:10

"Declare a holy fast;
*   call a sacred assembly.*
Summon the elders
*   and all who live in the land*
to the house of the Lord your God,
*   and cry out to the Lord."*
Joel 1:14

Dr. Phil, Dr. Oz, and Gayle King are three people who most of America know. Perhaps we don't want to know who they are, but we do. In one of my first years in ministry, Dr. Oz came to town to speak at a local club. I couldn't wait to see him. After all, he was famous and important, Oprah told me so. You know Oprah, of course. Everyone knows Oprah.

She is one of a handful of people who are known worldwide simply by a first name. For years, people would flock to the Oprah show to glean important information and be told and shown how to live better lives. Oprah had some real power. She still does, of course, but not as much. Yet, we still all know her by Oprah.

One of my favorite songs recently speaks to this phenomenon, it is a song called "What if his people prayed," from Casting Crowns:

What if the life that we pursue
Came from a hunger for the truth
What if the family turned to Jesus
Stopped asking Oprah what to do

I love this song. I thought about it while I was reading the book of Joel this morning. In the book, the people are called to a time of fasting and prayer. A time to remember who God is and what God will do. It will be a time of repentance and a time of grace. It won't be an easy time to turn away from the choices that they have made, but it must be done. In other words, it's time to live right, even if living right will be difficult.

The song always reminds me that the world may have suggestions and offer opportunities, but I need to keep my eye on God. Oprah is a wonderful person and has done remarkable things, but our hope comes from the one who made heaven and earth. The promises of that one are abundant life, not a quick fix or even a new car. (And you get a new car...and you get a new car).

What would happen if we turned to Jesus?
Are you ready to find out?

DAY 66 - BIGGER ISN'T ALWAYS BETTER.

Today's Reading Amos 9:11 – Nahum 3:19

He has shown you, O mortal, what is good.
    And what does the Lord require of you?
To act justly and to love mercy
    and to walk humbly[a] with your God.
Micah 6:8

We live in a world where sizzle matters. Big and splashy sells. Whether a big mansion or a big car, we have been conditioned to appreciate lavishness and size. It shouldn't be like that in the life of the church, but often it is the way. We look for the next big thing. We want bigger buildings. We want bigger choirs. We want bigger events. Lost in the search for bigger is a small word...WHY?

Why do we look for these things?
Why do we value these things?
Why do we think bigger is always better?
Why do we constantly search for more?

Perhaps our quest for bigger and better is some twisted attempt to please God. Perhaps our belief is that God is impressed with the size and with numbers. We might believe that God values the big and elaborate more than the small and simple. We might even think that God will reward us more if our event or ministry is just a little bit bigger.

As I was reading the passages this morning, I couldn't help but

be struck at these words from Micah:
What does the LORD require of you but to do justice, love kindness, and walk humbly with your God?

Notice what God is not requiring of us: Bigger...fancier...faster...louder...self-serving...numbers. When we are obedient to God. When we practice justice in a world that screams for justice, God is pleased. When we share kindness and find ways to love our neighbors, God is pleased. When we listen to God and walk with God and spend time with God, God is pleased.
What God wants is not numbers, and it is not flash; it is us! God wants to be in a relationship with us, wants to listen to us, and share with us. God wants us to share God's love with the world. Each one shares with one. Each one loves one. Those are the numbers God cares about. The kingdom grows through God's grace and the obedience of God's people.

Do you want bigger or are you searching for better?

DAY 67 - BUILDING UP

Today's Reading Habakkuk 1:1 – Zechariah 10:12

"I will strengthen them in the Lord
*   and in his name they will live securely,"*
declares the Lord
Zechariah 10:12

For the last 67 days, we have been reading through the Old Testament together. This is the final reading that will be dedicated strictly to the Old Testament. Tomorrow we move into the New Testament. So perhaps it's a time to review.

Our journey through the Hebrew Bible has been one of building foundations. We have looked at the stories we know so well. We started in the Garden of Eden and found ourselves on an ark with Noah. We journeyed with Abraham, Sarah, Isaac, Jacob, and Joseph. We read about the construction and reconstruction of the temple as we listened to the pleas of the prophets trying to bring the people back to God.

It has been a chance for us to learn about the need to depend upon God. Today's reading in Zechariah was a reminder of that need. We are a people in need of God. Despite our belief that we can do everything on our own, the Bible reminds us that we need God. We need a relationship with God. We need to turn back to God.

As we head into the New Testament, what has God shown you through the reading of the Old Testament?

DAY 68 - WHAT'S NEW?

Today's Reading Zechariah 11:1 – Matthew 4:25

Jesus went throughout Galilee, teaching in their synagogues, proclaiming the good news of the kingdom, and healing every disease and sickness among the people.
Matthew 4:23

God is always up to something. The question for us becomes do we want to join in on what God is doing? As we begin the reading in the Gospel of Matthew, we see what Jesus is up to. Jesus is teaching, preaching, and healing. Jesus is bringing the Gospel to the people.

Today's reading is an invitation. Jesus' ministry is about going to the people and meeting them where they are. This ministry needs co-laborers. The invitation for us is to join in the fun and join the ministry. Where there is need, here is where we are called to be.

It can be overwhelming and frustrating because there is so much need. So many things to do. So many good causes and great ways to help. What is the right thing to involve yourself in? Sometimes it is essential to start at the beginning. The following is a prayer that helps remind us it is all about Christ, an invitation to and an acknowledgment of Christ.

Christ Be With MeChrist with me, Christ before me, Christ behind me,
Christ in me, Christ beneath me, Christ above me,

Christ on my right, Christ on my left,
Christ where I lie, Christ where I sit, Christ where I arise,
Christ in the heart of everyone who thinks of me,
Christ in the mouth of everyone who speaks to me,
Christ in every eye that sees me,
Christ in every ear that hears me.
Salvation is of the Lord.
Salvation is of the Christ.
May your salvation, Lord, be ever with us.

St. Patrick

Let these words from St. Patrick many years ago be your words today.

DAY 69 – I LOVE ORANGE JUICE

Today's Reading Matthew 5:1 – Matthew 15:39

"Likewise, every good tree bears good fruit, but a bad tree bears bad fruit."
Matthew 7:17

I wrote this while Ginny and I were in Florida. I had a glass of fresh Florida orange juice in my hands. I love that juice. It has been a couple of years since we have been able to go down to Florida. Of all the things that I have miss about Florida, including Mickey Mouse, orange juice is top on the list.There is nothing quite like it for me. It is sweet. It smells great. It is the perfect complement to a nice cup of morning coffee. I love it.

In today's reading, we are reminded of the importance of good fruit. Jesus points out that a good tree provides good fruit. A bad tree? Well, that fruit isn't as good. Our words…our actions… these are the signs of the type of foundation we have.
When people spend time with you, what do they see? When they hang out with you, what do they hear? Are your actions that show your foundation based on God or betray a shaky foundation? What kind of fruit do you produce?

These words from Mother Theresa are powerful:

Dear Jesus,
Help us to spread your fragrance everywhere we go, flood our souls with your Spirit and life. Penetrate and possess our whole being so utterly that our lives may only be a radiance of yours.

Shine through us and be so in us that every soul we come in contact with may feel your presence in our soul. Let them look up and see no longer us but only Jesus. Stay with us, and then we shall begin to shine as you shine, so to shine as to be light to others. The light, O Jesus, will be all from you. It will be your shining on others through us. Let us thus praise you in the way you love best by shining on those around us. Let us preach you without words, but by our example by the catching force the sympathetic influence of what we do the evident fullness of the love our hearts bear to you.

-Mother Teresa

Living that type of life..that is good fruit indeed.

DAY 70 - WHAT REMAINS?

Today's Reading Matthew 16:1 – Matthew 26:56

"And someone came to Him and said, 'Teacher, what good thing shall I do so that I may obtain eternal life?'"
Matthew 19:16

We all know the story. We have read it, heard it, and perhaps even preached it. Jesus was talking to the young rich ruler about what is essential. I often thought at that moment when he left if he had one more unasked question for Jesus.

"If I give it all up…and give it away…what remains?"
It is a legitimate question. One that I am sure I would ask in the same situation. What do you think? What else remains?

I think the Gospels point to three things, Faith, Hope, and Love. These remain because they are characteristics of our Awesome God.

Trust God with what is and what will remain.

DAY 71 - IN MOTION

Today's Reading Matthew 26:57 – Mark 9:13

"Then Jesus went around teaching from village to village."
Mark 6:6

When I preach or even teach, I feel a need to be moving. I feel an energy that I do not typically have. I am so anxious and eager to share the Good News that was given to me that I am compelled to move. I think that is why it is always like coming home for me when I read the Gospel of Mark.

From the very beginning of the Gospel, we can sense the urgency. Jesus has a mission, and he must get going. The healings and teachings are non-stop. Jesus needs the world to hear his message about the kingdom of God. Just reading through the Gospel again gives me a sense of mission and a desire to go.

There is a world in need. People are hungry. People are sick, People are lost. People are broken. They need some good news; they need THE Good News. People don't want to wait for restoration. People are tired of being pushed out to the fringe.

What urgency is God placing on your heart? Where is God trying to use you in these urgent times? Can you feel the urgency in that call?

Get ready. Get set. Go!

DAY 72 - OUR LIPS ARE SEALED

Today's Reading Mark 9:14 – Luke 1:80

"Trembling and bewildered, the women went out and fled from the tomb. They said nothing to anyone, because they were afraid."
Mark 16:18

In 1981, the nation's youth were introduced to the Go-Go's. You could not escape their music when you turned on the radio or even the television. They were everywhere. The Go-Go's first hit that year was "Our lips are sealed." It was a catchy tune, and it spoke to the power of silence. Ignoring the names people call you. Ignoring the nonsense that people say. It was a song of empowerment trapped in a pop tune.

Silence can be a powerful thing. It can give us time to gather ourselves. It can stop you from saying something you will regret. It can also give others time to process the information before them. The world can use more quiet. Silence isn't always a good thing, however.

Sometimes we are silent because we are afraid. We may be quiet because we are too arrogant to speak as well. We see these two examples in our scripture reading today of silence. Throughout the Gospel of Mark, people are healed and told not to say anything, to be silent. They do not listen. They can't help to share the Good News.

At the Empty Tomb, the women told of Jesus' resurrection are instructed to tell everyone what has happened. We are told that they were afraid and stayed silent. In the Gospel of Luke, we read about Zechariah. He was a priest. He was married to Elizabeth. An angel appeared to him while he was in the temple and said he and Elizabeth would have a son. He did not believe it because they were old. Zechariah scoffed at the idea. Because of his arrogance, the angel said he would be unable to talk.

When has fear kept you from sharing the Good News? Perhaps you thought people would look at you funny. Maybe you thought you couldn't do it. When has arrogance kept you silent about the Good News? Perhaps you were with people who you thought should know better already. Maybe it was a matter of not wanting to spend time with a specific type of people.

Through the beautiful song stylings of the Go-Go's, we all know that there is a time for silence. Because of Mark Twain, we also know that perhaps the world will know we are a fool if we speak. The reality is that the Good News needs to be shared. If people think we are foolish for sharing it, that is okay. That is also okay if we need to spend time with folks and just "be there" for a while before sharing it. Everyone needs Jesus. We all need to tell the story.

Go Tell the Story.

DAY 73 - FEW OR MANY OR BOTH

Today's Reading Luke 2:1 – Luke 9:62

"About eight days after Jesus said this, he took Peter, John and James with him and went up onto a mountain to pray."
Luke 9:28

When I was attending St. John's elementary school, I remember wanting to be friends with everyone. Gus, Vince, Joe, Gino, Peter, Frank, Rich, Lisa, Linda, Holly, Krista, Diane, Christine, Angela, etc. It is really all I seemingly wanted, to be a part of everything and involved with everyone. I wanted everyone to be my BFF before we all knew what a BFF was.

In St. James high School, that changed, but just a little bit. I moved in different circles but still tried to and wanted to be friendly with everyone. Yet, as the years went on, I started to settle in with a core group of people. We would talk often. We would hang out all the time. We would get in trouble together. We would have fun together. Sometimes, we would get in trouble and have fun all at the same time.

My life has changed dramatically since those early school years. It has gotten busier and more complicated, Yet, some things have stayed the same. What I found to be so crucial in High School is still very important to me today; the circle.

We read about the circle today in the Gospel of Luke. Jesus is out telling the story of the kingdom; he is healing and raising people from the dead. People have really started following Jesus. From those people, he has chosen a circle of 12. Out of the circle of 12, Jesus has an inner circle of 3…Peter, James, and John.

Although Jesus spends a lot of time with his 12, he seemingly spends more time and more intimate time with the 3. He forms closer bonds and trusts them more. They are with him in his most vulnerable times. As we read today in the Transfiguration story, they are with him in some of the coolest and perplexing moments. No matter what, they are there. They depend on each other.

We all need to be part of the community. We need social interaction. This is vital to us. But, in addition, we all need that circle. The small group of people who are there with us through thick and thin. A group to share our highs and our lows. Amid the circle, we find peace, love, joy, and home.

Who is in your circle?

With who do you find that peace, love, joy, and home?

DAY 74 - KEEP IT STRAIGHT

Today's Reading Luke 10:1 – Luke 20:19

"Keeping a close watch on him, they sent spies, who pretended to be sincere. They hoped to catch Jesus in something he said, so that they might hand him over to the power and authority of the governor."
Luke 20:20

When I was a child, I went through a period where I had real trouble with the truth. Whenever I was faced with a difficult situation and was confronted, I took the easy way out and lied. As a young boy, I can remember several occasions when I met a bit of trouble; I would concoct some story to keep me safe.

Now, for the most part, these were minor things. I had not committed any crimes. I was often trying to just not get grounded or disciplined in some way. Sometimes the original lie would get me off the hook. I would think I was on top of the world. I had created the ultimate lie. However, things aren't always as they seem.

Inevitably, I would be put into a position where I needed to recall that original lie. I would need to remember it and keep it going. But, as I am sure you are aware, that did not always work. In fact, getting caught lying about the lie resulted in punishment far more significant than if I had just been honest from the beginning. Eventually, I learned that simply telling the truth is the easiest and most intelligent thing to do. No need to try to keep the lies in order; just tell the truth.

In the scripture reading today, Jesus is not trying to remember a lie, but his critics are trying to catch him up in his words. They are trying to trap him by using his words against him. They do not like the messages they hear and are bound and determined to stop him. Jesus knows this and yet does not change anything he was saying or doing.

Why?

Because Jesus is the Truth. His words were the very words of God. He spoke to a generation that needed to hear the Truth just as our generation needs to hear it.
Speak truth.
Seek Truth.

DAY 75 - LOOK AROUND

Today's Reading Luke 20:20 – John 5:47

"I have testimony weightier than that of John. For the works that the Father has given me to finish—the very works that I am doing—testify that the Father has sent me."
John 5:36

The days leading up to writing this reflection, I had spent a lot of time in the hospital. Yet, the reality is I am NOT a medical doctor. I am NOT a nurse. I am NOT an X-ray tech. Just hanging out in the hospital doesn't make me any of those things. Just claiming the title does not make me any of those things. Just wishing it to be true does not make me any of those things.

It takes training, commitment, and action. Today in the reading, we see Jesus speak to this reality. The people of Israel had been waiting for a Messiah for so long. They had been waiting and watching. Some had come before Jesus and had claimed to be Messiah, and some would come after him and claim to be him as well. Yet it was Jesus who was the one.

Jesus did not go around claiming the mantle. Instead, as he tells people in the Gospel of John, his doing the works of God proved who he was. Jesus would teach folks, but he did so much more than that. Jesus was with people. He healed, fed and people.

I claim to be a Christian. If I am not with the people, or do not feed the people or even if I do not love the people; it is all just words.

I want to be about more than words.
How about you?

DAY 76 - WHAT I WANT VERSUS WHAT I NEED

Today's Reading John 6:1 – John 15:17

"At this the Jews there began to grumble about him because he said, 'I am the bread that came down from heaven.' 'They said, Is this not Jesus, the son of Joseph, whose father and mother we know? How can he now say, I came down from heaven?'"
John 6:41-42

Not one of them. Not Best Smile, Cutest Couple, not Most Likely To Succeed. Definitely not Most Popular. Not one. I wanted one, any of them. High School was not exactly a crowning achievement of mine. So I wasn't surprised when the Year Book came out in my Senior Year, and I did not receive any superlatives. I wasn't surprised, but I know I felt it would have been nice to get just one.

Popularity is something we all don't get to experience. It is something that many of us wanted when we were younger, though. Sometimes perhaps we may feel the desire even as we mature. At the very least, we want to be liked, and that seems reasonable.

It had always fascinated me when I re-read this section of the Gospel of John. So we start today's reading by finding out Jesus had never been more popular. People were flocking from all over to see him and to hear him. They came to see miraculous signs and wonders. They came to experience his power and came to make him king.

It fascinates me that it was at this moment Jesus chose to deliver one of his most challenging teachings. I am the Bread of Life, Jesus said., Eat my flesh and live. Drink my blood and have everlasting life. These were not throwaway lines like they can become in a communion liturgy. Jesus was challenging them to understand what it meant that he was there. Jesus wanted them to understand what it meant to follow him.

How many of us would be willing to speak truth THAT bold when we are at our most popular at school, work, or home? How many of us would try to find a different way to say what needed to be said? Too often, it seems, I find myself focused on the wrong thing, the wrong kind of numbers.

Jesus gives us what we need. Jesus gives us Truth. He is not worried about popularity; Jesus is concerned about people. Jesus is committed to God the Father.

Are you?
Am I?

DAY 77 - THE JOB NEEDS DONE

Today's Reading John 15:18 – Acts 6:7

"In those days when the number of disciples was increasing, the Hellenistic Jews[a] among them complained against the Hebraic Jews because their widows were being overlooked in the daily distribution of food."
Acts 6:1

I look around me and see so much need. I read the news and am aware of so much trouble. When does it stop? Who is going to do something? These are just a couple of questions that I think of during times like these. None of us can do everything, yet we can all do something.
Isn't that the point? We all can do something. We have a particular talent, willingness, or the resources to accomplish things. Change happens when people who are capable of doing something actually do it. Yet, there is a danger that we all must be aware of.

The idea of doing something versus doing everything.

Everyone can do something, and we should. However, no one can do everything, nor should we try. In today's reading, we see a problem arise. A particular group of widows was seemingly not being treated as they should. The twelve were made aware of this problem. They did not actually make sure that these widows were being treated fairly each day. However, they ensured that there would be a group dedicated to doing just that.

The twelve knew that their gifts were in studying and proclaiming. They needed to focus on that. Yet, the need they were presented was real. They made sure that it was handled. Everyone can do something. When we all do what we are designed to do and called to do. Well, what can I say....We are unstoppable.

DAY 78 - WHY DO WE FORGET SO EASILY?

Today's Reading Acts 6:8 – Acts 16:37

" 'Surely not, Lord!' Peter replied. 'I have never eaten anything impure or unclean.' "
Acts 10:14

As parents, we spend a lot of time teaching our children what is good and bad. "Hot stove – bad"…" Kitty cat – good"…. "running with scissors – bad"…" coloring with crayons – good."
It is a never-ending battle at times. We try to raise our children and protect our children. Yet, there are always dangers just around the bend. So what do we do?

After all, that is the main question. How do we survive in a world that seems is poised to destroy us or self-destruct any minute? We learn a quick and efficient way to protect ourselves is by isolating ourselves from the danger. We create boxes for things and people. We put labels on those boxes. Once the boxes are labeled, we can then keep ourselves away from the dangerous boxes
.

The dangerous labels might look different for each of us, but we all seemingly have them. Over time we continue to isolate ourselves more and, moreover, the elusive safety we are seeking. This, for me, prompts the real question. Is this what life is supposed to be about?

This morning as I read the story of Peter and Cornelius, I couldn't help but think of this question. Peter and Cornelius were both good to me. They were doing what they were supposed to do. Living good lives, Godly lives. They were doing their part to follow Jesus Christ and be "storytellers" for the kingdom. Yet, these two men were isolated from each other because of ethnicity and station in life. They had been told, or tradition had been, that they could not fellowship together. They could not share a meal together.

Peter had forgotten the story of Creation. After the sixth day, God looks at what has been created and calls it "very good." There were no boxes. There was no isolation. God had deemed it all good. This deciding who was good and who was bad was a human creation. We turned from God and said, "We got this."

We are all guilty of forgetting. Forgetting God is God of all. God loves all. God desires all to be saved. God's love is available for all. We forget, or we don't like it. So let's spend some time today remembering. Let's remember who God is. Let us not forget the power of God's love.

Take some time today; remove one label from one box. Open yourself to the grace of God. Live like it is all "very good" indeed.

DAY 79 - WHAT CHOICE DO WE HAVE?

Today's Reading Acts 16:38 – Acts 28:16

"Before very long, a wind of hurricane force, called the Northeaster, swept down from the island. 15 The ship was caught by the storm and could not head into the wind; so we gave way to it and were driven along."
Acts 27: 14-15

I remember the day that I wrote this devotion. I woke up and though to myself "Happy Spring!" We had finally made it; perhaps it didn't seem likely but, we were there. However, in the part of the world I lived in, when I looked outside appeared that Mother Nature did not get the Spring memo...it was snowing. Again. Snow. In March. Would it ever end?

The snow would end at some point. The weather would break, and Spring would be here. There would be other storms, though, in the days and weeks ahead. It might be rain or wind, but either way, storms will come. We can't change that; all we can do is adapt, cope, and move on. This is the reality.

In today's readings, we are reminded of the inevitability of storms. Paul faced the storms as he was being sent to Rome. The storms were swift and severe. The storm threatened the lives of all those on board the ship. Yet, while all around him, people were freaking out, Paul remained steadfast. His confidence came not from being able to control the storm but from the peace that comes from knowing that the storm would not have the last word, God will.

We can't stop storms in our lives. They will happen. The ups and downs of life are part of life. What we need to do is focus on the One who is over even the storms. God will give us the confidence, peace, and strength that we need. We only need to trust Him.

Do you trust God is bigger than any storm?

DAY 80 - IT ALWAYS COMES BACK TO CLOWNS.

Today's Reading Acts 28:17 – Romans 14:23

For I am convinced that neither death nor life, neither angels nor demons,[k] neither the present nor the future, nor any powers, neither height nor depth, nor anything else in all creation, will be able to separate us from the love of God that is in Christ Jesus our Lord.
Romans 8: 38-39

For over three years while I was at Glassboro, I had spent a lot of time thinking about clowns. I spent a lot of time dreaming about clowns. I spent a lot of time planning for clowns. It always came back to clowns.

For me, C.L.O.W.N. (Creatively Loving Our Wonderful Neighbors) has become a powerful way to explain and live out the Big 2. You know the Big 2; Love God, Love others. It has been a way to try to create an environment where people can feel safe. Safe to share. Safe to laugh. Safe to be themselves. It is about building relationships and community. It is about understanding that God loves us and has claimed us as his own.

Reading the passage from today in Romans reminded me of that again. It was Paul's passionate pronouncement that NOTHING can separate us from the love of God. He writes that he is convinced. I love that. I need to hear that and ask myself, am I convinced? Do I live like I am convinced?

The sad reality for many that I have spent time with in my life is that they aren't convinced. The church and society have done such an excellent job of making them feel "less than." We need to change that. I need to change that, and you need to change that. Everyone matters. Everyone counts. Everyone is loved. No one is alone. These are simple statements, but they are also absolute truths in the eyes of the Truth.

So back to clowns I go. Praying for a plan. Praying for a vision. Praying for a possibility to help make a difference. Looking for ways to help create authentic community. Will you join me in this prayer?

DAY 81 - C'MON NOW...

Today's Reading Romans 15:1 – 1 Corinthians 14:40

" I thank God that I speak in tongues more than all of you. 19 But in the church I would rather speak five intelligible words to instruct others than ten thousand words in a tongue."
1 Corinthians 14:18

"I want you to come to our church today. I will be inside waiting for you. Once you go to the narthex and then into the sanctuary. You can sit in a pew in the nave. I will be up in the chancel. At first, talking to the pastor by the pulpit, and then I will have to get the elements for communion from the sacristy. I should be all done before the prelude starts. Oh, and by the way, bring the kids. We just love young people."

I have to be honest. I had to go online and read some of these terms up again. I know them; I just forget what many of them are. See, I have this little problem; I was born in 1966, not 1566, so much of this language is not natural for me. Of course, it is not for most people either. Yet, too often, the church tries to speak in tongues to a world that just isn't interested.

I realize that this is not the case for every person. I really do. I do know that it is the case for many. We assume they will understand why we stand when we play the benediction and bring up the MONEY to the altar. We think they will realize they need to read their bulletin and know when to stand and sing because the organ player will be playing immediately. The truth is there is just way too much assumption that goes on in the church.

In my experience, the repetition and old church language creates a subculture that is hard to decipher for many who may come to visit us on Sundays. There is a seeming expectation that people will have to adapt to us and learn our language and customs and learn them independently.

Now, I know this is not what Paul is peaking about in his letter to the people of Corinth when he talks about speaking in tongues in today's reading. I get it. However, he is really referencing order in worship. I would suggest that nothing "order-ish" happens when some of your people do not know what is going on or are trying to decipher your language.

All things to all people is what Paul writes. Shouldn't we at least try a little harder?
See ya at church!

DAY 82 - NOW WOULD BE GOOD

Today's Reading 1 Corinthians 15:1 – Galatians 3:25

"I do not set aside the grace of God, for if righteousness could be gained through the law, Christ died for nothing!"
Galatians 2:21

I remember several years ago, I officiated the funeral of a 23-year-old young man. He was a father of twins. All throughout the funeral, my attention was on the twins. They looked so innocent. They seemed to not have a care in the world. All around them, people were crying and devastated, but it was not impacting them yet.

In many ways, I think we are often like those children. All around us, there is a need. All around us, there is pain. We walk around like nothing is happening unless it is impacting us directly. When a child is hungry, she cries. When he is unhappy, he cries. A child only responds when there is a perceived personal urgent need. Are we like that?

Do we only think about the poor when we see a homeless person on the street or see a commercial about starving children? Do we only think of war when we see the news or read about Afghanistan ? Do we only think of racism when we see things on the news? Do we only think of police officers and other first responders when we see something terrible that has happened?

Often times we live our lives in reactionary ways. Something, usually wrong, happens, and then we respond. In today's reading, Paul is telling the people and us that the Gospel is urgent. It needs to be lived out. It does not need to wait for something to happen. Something has already happened. Jesus!

Jesus has given us the way. He has shown us the truth and provided us life. Because of Jesus, Paul could endure all he did to continue to live out the Story. Because of Jesus, we are called to live out that same story.

It is urgent!
It does matter!
Tell the story!

DAY 83 - THAT'S WHY

Today's Reading Galatians 3:25 – Colossians 4:18

"And whatever you do, whether in word or deed, do it all in the name of the Lord Jesus, giving thanks to God the Father through him."
Colossians 3:17

Every parent has done it. We swear we will never do it. We will be "better" than our parents. We think we will do things differently. We have good intentions, the best of intentions. Yet, without fail, we do it, and it feels good…for a second. Yes, eventually, we all tell our kids, "because I told you so."

I remember hearing my parents tell me that and thinking that is simply not good enough; I need more. I DESERVE more. I want an explanation. It doesn't make sense; there has to be some hidden reason. I was never satisfied with that answer and swore I would never use it with my children.

We all know how this story ends. Of course, I did use it with my children and probably more than once. How often can I sit down in the back of the car and explain why you need to do that? How many times can I offer up the same explanation for picking up the toys before bedtime? How long, oh Lord??????

Now that wasn't always how I answered my children. I did try to explain the reason behind the "why." I did try to be an example to them and show them that mom and dad weren't just saying these things; they lived these things. We were polite and caring. We took the time to be nice to others, respectful, and went to church. We lived our lives like a belief in Jesus really matters.

I did these things and hoped and prayed. I prayed that the lessons would connect. I prayed that the "why" would sink in. I pray that my kids will see the power of living fruitful lives, faithful lives, good lives, as Paul writes about in today's readings. I prayed that our example could show our kids that there is another way. The world doesn't get to decide what is essential in your life... you do. The world may gossip, lie, and cheat and live a life that brings praise to immorality, but you do not have to.

My parent's example connected with me. My wife's example connected with me. The life, death,
and resurrection of Jesus Christ connected with me. This is what I want for my kids. This is what I want for the world.

So yea...because I said so.
That's why!

DAY 84 - STAY AWAY FROM IT

Today's Reading 1 Thessalonians 1:1 – Philemon 1: 25

"Timothy, my son, I am giving you this command in keeping with the prophecies once made about you, so that by recalling them you may fight the battle well, 19 holding on to faith and a good conscience, which some have rejected and so have suffered shipwreck with regard to the faith."
1 Timothy 1: 18-19

Some people thrive in chaos. I am not one of them. Some people are fed by turmoil and upheaval in their lives. I am not one of them. The world is made up of many different types of people. I would venture a guess that many of those types reside on your Facebook timeline. Go ahead, take a look. I'll wait.

Paul's writings in scripture are filled with warnings to stay away from a particular behavior. These behaviors will steal time from you, time that should be directed towards God. Paul's warnings have been white noise for me recently, until today. Today, as I read, I was struck by his call to give someone who causes controversy/trouble a chance, but if they continue that behavior, to distance yourself from them. Today, this struck home.

How much time is wasted dealing with trouble created and perpetuated by a single person and their negativity? How much time is spent dealing with the drama that has been created by someone else's bad choices or attitude? What is the cost for me to spend time in those situations with people like that?

I exercise several times a week because I want to do what I can to get fit and stay healthy. If I care about my physical health that much, shouldn't I be just as concerned with my mental and spiritual health? I have to be better. I need to make space.

Paul's writings to Timothy were in part a reminder to Timothy of who he was and what he was called to do. It was a reminder that God had a plan for Timothy and that he needed to focus on the agenda and not be sucked into other people's stuff. I believe God has a plan for me as well. I need to be faithful to that plan and stay away from the drama.

My prayer this morning is that I can move in that direction. My prayer this morning for you is that you can move towards that if you are dealing with these same issues.

DAY 85 - AM I A GOSSIP?

Today's Reading Hebrews 1 – James 3:12

"The tongue also is a fire, a world of evil among the parts of the body. It corrupts the whole body, sets the whole course of one's life on fire, and is itself set on fire by hell."
James 3:6

"Did you hear?"
How many conversations you have been part of recently have started out with that or a similar question?
"Can you believe it?"

Have you found yourself saying this to someone recently? Have you had someone say this to you?

Now maybe you are different from me. Perhaps you have not had any recent conversation that started out with one of these two or a similar question. If that is so, then good for you. You can go on about your day. What follows is for the rest of us....myself included.
Why do we do it? Why do we allow ourselves to be sucked into the negative conversation?

These questions are essential. These questions need to be addressed. We may think that gossip is normal or not gossip if it is accurate; however, we would be missing the point.
Spending time gossiping is not only a waste of time, but it is harmful. It allows us to view people as "less than." It is a way in which we can demean someone and feel good about ourselves

simultaneously. In the scripture today, James thought that it was destructive enough to address. James spoke about the power of the tongue.

The tongue gives us the power to tear down but also to lift up. It is just as easy for us to speak love to people as gossip, so let's talk about love. Let us use our tongues today to pray for each other. Let us use our words to compliment each other. Let us use our words today to instruct each other and encourage each other. Let us be speakers of love.

DAY 86 - TEACH THEM WELL

Today's Reading James 3:13 – 3 John 14

"Be shepherds of God's flock that is under your care, watching over them—not because you must, but because you are willing, as God wants you to be; not pursuing dishonest gain, but eager to serve; not lording it over those entrusted to you, but being examples to the flock."
1 Peter 5: 2-3

My family is filled with people involved in education. We have former school board members, teachers, school nurses, and administrators. Education has always been very important in our family. It is something to this day that I value immensely. Perhaps it is why at the age of 48, I am still in school.

Yet, not all teachers are created equally, and not all educators have been created from the same mold. It is simply a reality. So what makes the difference? Why are some "better" than others? Why are some teachers and educators at a different level? Well, maybe I can answer that with an example.

One of my favorite professors in seminary was Dr. Craig Keener. Craig was one of the most brilliant men that I had ever met, but that wasn't why he was my favorite. Craig explained the most difficult pieces of the New Testament in ways even I could understand, but that wasn't why he was my favorite professor. Instead, Craig was my favorite professor because of his genuine love of us, the world, and God. Story after story that was shared with us showed Craig to be a teacher, leader, and a "doer" of the Word. He was a living example to us because of his compassion and love.

In today's reading, Peter urges the shepherds to be a good example to not lead out of necessity but out of a genuine desire and love. We all have to wrestle with going through the motions at times, no matter what we do. Peter's words and Dr. Keener's example are a constant reminder to me to care for and be there for people.

If people can't see me living out the words I say, I waste everyone's time. Crosby, Stills, Nash, and Young have a great song called "Teach the Children Well". The song is a reminder to "feed them on your dreams." Feed the children and feed each other on the dreams that we have of a better world. The dreams of when god's will be done here like it is in heaven. The dreams of a place where we do all live together and love together and help together.

Teach. Learn. Love. Live. Amen.

DAY 87 - THE END IS COMING

Today's Reading Jude 1 – Revelation 7:17

"For the Lamb at the center of the throne
will be their shepherd;
he will lead them to springs of living water.
And God will wipe away every tear from their eyes."
Revelation 7:17

Several years ago,, we went to see a local High School production of the "Wizard of Oz." The Wizard of Oz is a great story, and I remember watching it as a little child. Every year when it came on TV, I was excited and afraid. I was excited to see my "friends" once again. I was worried because I knew the flying monkeys and the wicked witch were coming.

I couldn't take my eyes away from the screen; I would smile as we met the munchkins yet again and sing the songs. Yet, I knew that this joy would end soon because of that blasted witch and her flying monkeys. No matter what, I kept watching. I couldn't take my eyes off the screen.

Why would I put myself through that as a child? Why would I stick through even when things didn't look so good? It is because I knew the end of the story. I knew like Dorothy would learn that there is no place like home! The good guys were going to win. I didn't want to miss that.

I haven't read through the Book of Revelation as many times as I have read other parts of the bible. It is not my "favorite" book,

Yet, as I was reading it today, all I could think about was the Wizard of Oz. There is a lot of bad things happening in the book. Some things seem much worse than flying monkeys and wicked witches. Yet, I still kept reading. Why?

In part because I am DETERMINED to finish what I started on January 1st (who is with me?).

However, the most important reason is that I know the end of the story, and so do you. It is a story of newness and majesty. It is a story of community and relationship. It is a story of love and forgiveness. It is a story of forever. It is the story of us…and God together.

There is, in fact, no place like home…and that home is with God. Now that is a happy ending.

DAY 88 - GOD'S IN CHARGE

Today's Reading Revelation 8:1 - 12:17

But in the days when the seventh angel is about to sound his trumpet, the mystery of God will be accomplished, just as he announced to his servants the prophets.
Revelation 10:7

I have read these chapters four times now. I struggle with what to say. What wisdom can I offer? The words are all blending together and creating dark images in my mind. Yet, there is one thing that remains true, and that truth is God. I feel an assurance that even in the confusion I feel tonight that God is working.

Together we are drawing closer to the end of our journey. In many ways this journey has been way more than 90 days already. This is a project that I started several years ago. In the midst of all that was happening in life there has been many starts and stops along the way. Yet, in my chaos, God remains steadfast.

I encourage to take a moment today and reflect. Did any of this seem possible? How could we do this? It was such a huge commitment and life was so busy and unpredictable. Yet, here we are. So close to the end and through it all God was with us.

God is with us and God is in charge.

DAY 89 - SEEING GOD

Today's Reading Revelation 13:1 - 17: 18

"Then I looked, and there before me was the Lamb, standing on Mount Zion"
Revelation 14:1

It is about 10 p.m., and I am sitting in my office trying to finish up my writing for the night. I have been so busy and focused tonight that I needed to take a little break. So I went downstairs and was sitting with Ginny and watched her at work. She was doing some crafting, and it was mesmerizing. She showed so much patience, creativity, and love in doing what she was doing.

At that moment, I understood today's reading. The prophet was given a vision of God. God in the midst of all that was happening. God was at work with patience, creativity, and love. God was and is at work. We have talked about it throughout this journey together. Yet, it was in watching my wife work that it became real again.

I have made it through this journey because of her. She has been the hands, eyes, and voice of God throughout every moment. She has given me the courage and encouragement to do what I did not think I could do. I have quit on myself so many times, but she never has, and for that, all I can say is thank you. You are reading this today because God used Ginny in powerful ways. I have been blessed to see and experience it.

Where do you see God today?

DAY 90 - WE DID IT!

Today's Reading Revelation 18:1 – Revelation 22:21

"He who testifies to these things says, "Yes, I am coming soon."
Amen. Come, Lord Jesus.
The grace of the Lord Jesus be with God's people. Amen."
Revelation 22: 20-21

Well, we have done it. It seemed like an impossibility on January 1st, but here we are. 90 days, and we have gone from Genesis through Revelation. We have read about Adam, Noah, Moses, and Abraham. We have heard stories about Ruth, Esther, Miriam, and Mary. Along the way, we have uncovered some things and reimagined some of the old stories.
Today's reading was a warning and a promise. A sign that choosing to ignore God has consequences. It is also a promise that God is not done with us yet. God is doing a new thing. God is at play. God is creating. I want a part of that new thing. I want to play with God. I want to create with God.

We end the Bible in the same place we started it, dwelling with God. There is no better place to be. We may be done reading through the bible THIS time, but our journey through the word will continue.

Conclusion -

Wow! We did it. I know it didn't seem possible. I am sure somewhere around the book of Leviticus, it became tedious, but you kept going. You probably felt like Job a few times listening to his friends assail him and wondering if there was another way to get the job done. But friends, you did it.

Now, what do you do? Do not stop. Keep going and draw closer to God. Continue to spend time in God's word. This is what I am sure of, God did not bring you this far to abandon you. Your journey with God is just starting. I can't wait to hear from you about what is next. Please take a moment and send me an email at pastorbluejeans@me.com and tell me what you thought of the journey.

Keep your eyes out, I am already following God's lead and working on my next book.

Made in the USA
Middletown, DE
16 September 2021

47607635R00104